DARE TO FAIL

DARE TO FAIL

JAMES HWANG

Dare to Fail

Copyright © 2024 by James Hwang

Published by: Bexsi Publishing
All rights reserved.

Disclaimer: This book contains many stories of real-life situations. Some names and specific events have been changed to safeguard privacy.

No part of this book may be reproduced, stored in a retrieval system, or transmitted by any means, electronic, mechanical, photocopying, recording, or otherwise, without written permission from the author.

ISBN-13: 978-1-961987-02-9

TABLE OF CONTENTS

Preface 7
Introduction 11
    Why You Should Dare to Fail. 11
Chapter 1. Immigrant Mentality 21
    Surviving In an Unfamiliar Land. 22
    English As My Ticket to The World. 24
    Acceptance Arrives When You Deliver Value. 29
Chapter 2. Ambitions to Change the World. 35
    Grit Sets You Apart 36
    The Two Faces of Hazing. 40
    Poor Grades Can Make the Man 47
    Hwangisms Introduced: Land the Boat 51
Chapter 3. The Ugly Truth of Glory. 53
    Reality Sometimes Has Teeth 55
    The Tip of the Spear. 58
    Quite Like Mayday 60
Chapter 4. The Smartest Person in the Room Syndrome. .. 65
    Making the Transition 66
    A New Path. 68
    Learn From Failed Assumptions. 71
    Hwangism: "Reach Around to the Other Side" 75
Chapter 5. Dollars and Downfall 77
    The Right of Way That Led Me Astray 80
    A Time to Print More Money 87

	It Gets Worse 90
	Just In Time Redemption 94

Chapter 6. **The East/West Conundrum** 101
    Good Move 102
    East Camp Vs West Camp 104

Chapter 7. **The Secret Sauce to Effective Execution** 113
    A New Dawn 116
    Hwangism: Seven Times Four Different Ways 124

Chapter 8. **The First Executive (Dis)Appointment** 131
    Where's the Money Going? 132
    Execution Is Everything 140

Chapter 9. **Cars and Coming of Age** 143
    Look Before You Leap 145
    Family Fails 151

Chapter 10. **Being Invited to Try Again** 157

Chapter 11. **Gaps in Leadership** 169

Chapter 12. **Making the Difficult but Right Decision** 179
    Hwangisms Continued 192

Chapter 13. **When You Overstayed Your Welcome** 195
    More Hwangisms 200

Chapter 14. **Leadership Framework** 201

Conclusion 209

Sources 213

PREFACE

"For a just man may fall seven times and rise again."
 (Proverbs 24:16)

In today's social media-fueled environment, public opinion vis-a-vis the number of "likes" received from loosely labeled "friends," or "connections" can determine the success or failure of projects, initiatives and personal efforts. If an event is circulated on social media and is deemed successful, others will be quick to create momentum and expand the positive notions "virally." However, in the event that we consider an action a failure, there is no empathy or comprehension. There is minimal patience in cyberspace. We render judgement quickly and the momentum of group think accelerates the "dislikes" to a point where the digital realm creates a "cancel culture" approach to people, events, actions and initiatives. "Cancel culture" is the social media's version of conducting a trial through a public court of opinion but it can also be riddled with cyber bullying, harassment, and even personal attacks. Such a whirlpool of judgements can dictate failure but more so, it leaves the contributor of the adjudicated action embarrassed, demotivated and defeated. Such severe mental consequences of failures limits the aspiring generations of leaders and followers. It seems that the only acceptable outcome is perfection or mass "likes." Our need for immediate gratification renders the concept of learning, adaptation, perseverance and iterative improvement as a forgotten art.

Even in religious teachings, we are taught that righteous and just people will fail, and failure is a prerequisite to wisdom. Those that consistently and quickly fail, and learn from their mistakes, allow growth, maturity and most importantly, wisdom to transpire. Our current middle and front line managers endeavor to become successful in their roles but very few managers actually become leaders. Leaders must understand and know how to build a relationship, enhance trust and become the mentors for the next cohort of leaders. Learning how to build a relationship, or figuring out how to work together is an iterative process. There is no answer key or panacea.

This book was written to remind us that failure is something we should not "cancel." Rather, failure is a normal course of life. Imperfection, missteps and even failures are not just acceptable, but they should be embraced. Maya Angelou teaches that, ***"you may encounter many defeats, but you must not be defeated. In fact, it may be necessary to encounter the defeats, so you can know who you are, what you can rise from, how you can still come out of it."*** In essence, failures allow each of us to learn, persevere, and gain value. I wholeheartedly agree with Angelou.

I have made more than my fair share of mistakes. In fact, my failures would be multiple or exponential in comparison to what is commanded in the Book of Proverbs. However, once I was able to recognize that failures equate to knowledge and wisdom, I embraced and welcomed failure. In fact, I almost dared myself to fail so that I could learn and improve.

Lastly, although I discuss my professional failures throughout this book, there is an area that is even more important: the failures and missteps that I made as a parent and a husband. Without my family's perseverance and forgiveness, I would not have had the opportunity to build and rebuild my relationships with my wife and my children. As I reflect, I was not the very best husband or father. Notwithstanding my son and daughter's patience and "sticktuitiveness," I would not have had the opportunities to build and rebuild trust by doing things together even though I was not the most patient teacher or coach. My wife's strong Christian foundation and beliefs allowed me to make mistakes and she prayed awfully hard on my behalf. What I learned from my wife is how to be a mentor. She was able to teach me to become a mentor as I have spent the last three decades as her apprentice. I am still making mistakes, but I am getting closer to success. The more I am able to embrace failures and missteps, the more wisdom and improvement I am able to gain. My ask for each of the readers is to embrace my failures and missteps as the first step towards accepting your failures, shortcomings and mistakes and learn from them and become successful because of them!

All the best!
—James

INTRODUCTION

WHY YOU SHOULD DARE TO FAIL

I stood at the podium, staring out at the crowd. Men in business suits and women in brightly colored dresses were sitting and staring back at me from the depths of the auditorium; there were fifty or so. We had all been through the ceremony that most American immigrants dream of: naturalization. More than a mere formality, our certificate embodies the assurance that our new country is committed to providing us with the freedom to achieve higher goals.

I had not prepared for the speech, but that did not mean I was not qualified to give it. I was enrolled in West Point, the training ground for future presidents, generals, and leaders of business. West Point was a few other things, too, but we'll get to that in a minute.

The master of ceremonies introduced me as the guest speaker. Personally, I didn't think a graduating high school senior like me had the qualifications. I had little time to prepare what I was going to say, so I fell back on the familiar narrative.

To start, I thanked God and my new country. With this, I was sure I was speaking on behalf of everyone. Otherwise, they wouldn't have turned up at that auspicious event.

Next, I emphasized things one would normally say in similar circumstances such as:

"Today is just a starting point. Everyone in this room with me is bound for great things!"

"We are going to pick up the standard and run forward, into the fray."

While those words were heartfelt, I played it safe to avoid errors and conceal my lack of preparation. If I could go back in time, I might have picked a different subject.

Failure.

As a kid, I failed at sports, until I found American football. During my first year at West Point, I navigated a series of challenges before understanding the system, which eventually allowed me to progress and join the ranks of the upperclassmen. In the early years of my career, I failed at communicating with frontline workers, and later failed at communicating with upper management. But I learned from each of those experiences and grew as a leader.

Coming in as a very young immigrant from Asia, I had this conundrum. Should I be that kid who was expected to be good in math like every other Asian? Or should I be part of a varsity team so I could fit in? Interestingly enough, if I had a distinct advantage over the other kids, it was that I was quite sharp in mathematics (I know what you're thinking). But I wanted to fit in, and math was not the way to do it. In my attempt to be like the cool American-born kids, I focused more on making it in the football team, and less on my academic standing. I did make it to the varsity team but my grades leading up to college suffered. In order to qualify for college, my guidance counselor encouraged me to take the SATs.

It turned out that my grades, although not quite stellar, *were* good enough, and the next thing I knew, I was perusing a packet from Princeton. As I was reading the acceptance letter, my eyes darted to the tuition fees section. I had supposed my parents could afford paying $50,000 for my college tuition fees for all four years. I was about to approach them when I had a hard look again at the letter. It was not for the four years...it was PER YEAR! Given our family's limited financial resources, I refrained from discussing the matter with my parents. It did not help that I did not seek scholarship opportunities.

By the time I was seriously looking at colleges it was too late. As an immigrant, growing up in a struggling lower income family, fifty grand a year might as well have been fifty million. My uncle, who was in the military, suggested I apply to West Point.

Securing admission to West Point required obtaining glowing recommendations from influential individuals, a prospect that seemed overwhelming given my lack of connections. The challenge was to persuade a congressperson or senator to vouch for me. At that time, Phil Gramm represented my interests in the Senate, and I surmise that Wendy Gramm, his wife, may have played a supportive role. With her academic credentials from Northwestern University and her distinction as the daughter of a pioneering Korean-American officer in a U.S. sugar cane company, her influence could have been significant.

Those helping hands added up. I got admitted to the U.S. Military Academy at West Point. However, my admission was contingent on becoming a U.S. citizen, which I received just in time for the start of the program.

It would be tough to name another American institution as intrinsically connected to cultivating successful leaders as West Point. Founded in 1802, and known more formally as the United States Military Academy, it prides itself on a 47-month leader-development program. This program is "steeped in academic rigor, military discipline, and physical challenges, all built upon a moral-ethical foundation," reflecting the ethos West Point upholds in its core messages. The academy takes understandable pride in the fact that "today's cadets will become tomorrow's military, public, and private-sector leaders."[1]

In addition to Ulysses S. Grant and Robert E. Lee — the Civil War's most famous opposing generals — West Point grads include General John J. Pershing, Brigadier General Douglas MacArthur, General George Patton, and President (and former general) Dwight D. Eisenhower. West Point successes are not limited to the military. Astronauts including Edwin E. "Buzz"

---

1 "About West Point," United States Military Academy: West Point. *https://www.westpoint.edu/leadership-center/mcdonald-leadership-conference/about-west-point*

Aldrin, Edward White II, and Michael Collins along with current astronauts Robert (Shane) Kimbrough and Andrew R. Morgan all list West Point on their resumes. So does former Twitter (now X) CFO Anthony Noto along with Joe DePinto and Alex Gorsky, the CEOs of 7-Eleven and Johnson & Johnson, respectively.

Yet West Point is also one of the first places where I learned the value of failure.

Many view failure as a detriment, the least desirable of all outcomes. Consider all those modifying adjectives: *colossal* failure, *monumental* failure, *abject* failure. Think of that cautionary slogan: *People don't plan to fail; they fail to plan.*

People are haunted by past failures. They ruminate over decades-old mistakes that culminate into a series of traumas holding them back from achieving their full potential. As an entrepreneur and business leader, I have seen how often businesses avoid failure like the plague.

Our approach to failure is often misguided; instead of offering support, we tend to penalize it. This perspective is flawed. It's crucial to foster an environment where failure can be openly discussed and addressed. We should focus on resolving failures rather than penalizing them, because success is often preceded by, guess what, a series of failures.

Frederick Banting's early career was a litany of failures. His medical practice barely paid the rent. He was nearly fired several times from an assistant professorship. Eventually, his fiancée called off their wedding. A few years later, he discovered insulin. He remarked that, "I am a firm believer in the theory that you can do or be anything that you wish in this world, within reason, if you are prepared to make the sacrifices, think and work hard enough and long enough."[2]

I would add that you also have to welcome, embrace, and even celebrate failure.

Penicillin, famously, was the result of a messy scientist named Alexander Fleming rushing out of his lab for an extended holiday. He returned to find an uncovered Petri dish of staphylococcal bacteria (the source of deadly staph infections) contaminated with mold spores. Fleming soon realized the mold was killing the bacteria. That mold was part of the *Penicillium* genus and led to his discovery of penicillin. Or as he humbly put it, "I did not invent penicillin. Nature did that. I only discovered it by accident."[3]

Even that success seemed like failure because it would be over a decade before penicillin was widely used. While I'm amused at the relevance of the saying, "We believe in science," a totally synonymous statement would be, "We believe in failure."

On October 4, 1957, Americans awoke to huge headlines and frantic radio broadcasts informing them the Soviets had successfully launched their Sputnik satellite — beating the U.S. in the space race. Yet that crisis and the failure that it implied drove President John F. Kennedy to encourage the country to put a person on the moon before 1970. The dream outlived him.

---

2   Pramuk, Jacob. "Police: McClendon Crashed Traveling at 'High Rate of Speed,'" CNBC. March 4, 2016. *https://www.cnbc.com/2016/03/02/ex-chesapeake-ceo-mcclendon-dies-in-car-wreck-day-after-indictment.html*

3   Tan, Siang Yong, Jason Merchant and Yvonne Tatsumura. "Alexander Fleming (1881-1955): Discoverer of penicillin." *Singapore Medical Journal* vol. 56,7 (2015): 366-7. *https://www.ncbi.nlm.nih.gov/pmc/articles/PMC4520913/*

Supported by Congress and the American people, undeterred by innumerable failures and even tragic losses of life, the country succeeded — beating Kennedy's deadline by months. Today, a trio of billionaires (Bezos, Branson, and Musk) are engaged in a private race to space, piercing the atmosphere with rocket ships launched in part from the debris of failure. Since I suspect most readers are either entrepreneurs, executives, or aspiring to be one or the other, I'll conclude with a few examples from the world of business.

When Harland David Sanders retired, he was flat broke. He survived, thanks to a $105-a-month Social Security check. He ran a boat business that failed, and while his restaurant was succeeding, it was tucked inside a gas station and hardly raking in cash. He had a unique, tasty recipe for fried chicken, but he got rejected again and again when he tried to sell his concept. Eventually, however, he was able to franchise his ideas and become the man we know today as Colonel Sanders. Today, KFC is part of the billion-dollar, multinational YUM corporation.

In his early thirties, Sam Walton owned a single Newport, Arkansas based Ben Franklin store (a discount retailer). Across a six-state region, Walton's Ben Franklin outsold every other store in the company. Although he owned the franchise and had a talent for selling, he didn't own the lease. Witnessing Walton's success firsthand, his landlord tried to buy the business for his son. When Walton refused to sell, the landlord refused to renew his lease.

Although Walton eventually opened other stores, his hard work wasn't producing sufficient profits. Aggressive discounting requires volume and when he brought his ideas for cost-cutting to Ben Franklin executives, they refused to back him. Undeterred, he mortgaged his house and borrowed money to open Wal Mart Discount City in 1962. The rest is history.

I could say the same thing about Walt Disney, who was fired because "he lacked imagination and had no original ideas." He saw his first animation company go bust and then was turned down for financing hundreds of times before opening Disney World. Bill Gates's first computer company failed. Henry Ford had two failed car companies and nothing but debt, yet he still managed to found Ford Motor Company.[4]

An old saying warns that experience is what you get when you don't get what you want. The experience of failure does more than develop character. It can actually help you develop a superpower: *resiliency*. Of course, you need to examine your failures and figure out how to recalibrate, so you'll succeed the next time. But the most important thing is to acknowledge how vital failure is in the process of growth. Every failure is a potential lesson. Without my numerous failures, I wouldn't be here right now. I wouldn't have led three successful businesses. Nor would I have the drive and self-confidence to pursue a PhD in middle age.

If you haven't succeeded, it may be because you haven't failed enough. This is why I am writing about my own failures. Because I believe that if you learn to embrace failure — and learn from it — you can become the success story you have always dreamed of.

---

4   Kumar, Jayant. "13 Business Leaders Who Failed Before They Succeeded," LinkedIn. May 14, 2016. *https://www.linkedin.com/pulse/13-business-leaders-who-failed-before-succeeded-jayant-kumar*

No doubt the next generation of leaders can do even better. In fact, they must. Unfortunately, mentorship and coaching are non-existent or minimal at best in the current business culture. If you have a great mentor, acknowledge your blessings. Consider paying it forward and seeking someone else to coach. You'll find you learn as much, if not more, as a teacher than you will as a student.

My sincere hope is that you read about my mistakes with an open heart and an open mind. Learn from them. Adapt them to your style. Together we can advance our next generational workforce by giving them a leader they deserve: YOU!

CHAPTER 1

IMMIGRANT MENTALITY

Many immigrants arrive in the United States having overcome tremendous adversities. Their circumstances are often shaped by severe economic and political difficulties including terrorism, crime, poverty, and disease. In many cases, they came from societies where prosperity is reserved for a privileged few, leaving the majority to contend with stark deprivation.

Money won't buy happiness, but studies confirm people in poor countries are less satisfied than those in affluent ones. It is easy for privileged people to dismiss economic concerns. Financial distress is a contributing factor in everything from drug and alcohol abuse to divorce and suicide. Money is not everything but losing a job or losing a home can often drive someone to the brink of despair.[5]

---

5   Glei, Dana A, and Maxine Weinstein. "Drug and Alcohol Abuse: The Role of Economic Insecurity." *American Journal of Health Behavior*, vol. 43,4 (2019): 838-853. doi:10.5993/AJHB.43.4.16. *https://www.ncbi.nlm.nih.gov/pmc/articles/PMC6631323/*
"Money Ruining Marriages in America," Ramsey Solutions. February 6, 2018. *https://www.ramseysolutions.com/company/newsroom/releases/money-ruining-marriages-in-america*
Zapata, Kimberly. "Financial Stress Is a Leading Catalyst for Suicide — Here's How You Can Find Help," *Health.* August 25, 2021. *https://www.health.com/money/financial-stress-suicide-risk*

SURVIVING IN AN UNFAMILIAR LAND

I'm proud to be from South Korea. Yet I arrived here a failure, having endured the aftermath of the Korean War which depressed my home country's standard of living for decades. While most Americans would describe my birthplace as a democracy, from 1961 to 1979 it was ruled by President Park Chung-hee, a dictator who brought our country down. Although he oversaw a period of unprecedented economic growth, he regularly cracked down on protestors, used the military to murder dissidents, and trampled on the most basic of civil liberties like free speech and freedom of the press.

I remember using an outhouse instead of an indoor restroom and playing with a decrepit soccer ball. In spite of that, I also remember early childhood as a time free from responsibilities. I enjoyed lax discipline because I lived with my aging grandmother, playing in the streets late at night when the TV stopped broadcasting. My parents were busy working, so my "Harmony" (Korean for grandmother) was the caretaker. There was also my German uncle who married my aunt and paved the way for our eventual immigration. I was just six years old when we arrived in the United States.

I had never been on an airplane before. We landed in Honolulu, Hawaii — my point of entry to America. What I remember is more exasperation than relief as we boarded a small bus after we landed, which began going round and round the airport in seemingly endless circles. For many arrivals from other countries, that "Wiki Wiki" shuttle is their first introduction to the United States, followed by an even longer and less pleasant experience.

I am not certain if we were among the first to disembark, but I do know that anyone with a U.S. passport was directed to the right and sped through the process. We went to the left where I was fingerprinted and briefly interviewed. It was all incredibly overwhelming for a young boy who had never left South Korea.

They kept telling me we were in Hawaii, but that sounded like a mythical place from a storybook. All I had really witnessed was the interior of a 747's fuselage, the "Wiki Wiki" shuttle, and the airport. It felt as though we were in that shuttle forever. As you will soon discover, I now possess a bit of well-earned hostility toward tiny buses.

Eventually, we walked back onto the tarmac, climbed the stairs and, much to my dismay, got on another plane. This was the one that would take us to Los Angeles. At LAX (Los Angeles International Airport), my uncle and aunt rented a large cargo van for us and all of our possessions. I like to joke that my earliest recollections of the mainland U.S. were being kidnapped and loaded into a beige, Ford Econoline 150. It had no windows and no rear air conditioning. Our family was sitting in the back on the cold and rusty floor. This was my earliest experience in the U.S., not quite what I hoped for based on how I imagined America would be. However, I still enjoyed being inside a motorized vehicle, in a new country, basking beneath the balmy Southern California sunshine. How could I complain?

Little did I know, the destination was Ft. Hood outside of Killeen, Texas.

ENGLISH AS MY TICKET TO THE WORLD

I remember random images from my very first road trip, standing up in the rear of the cargo van, peering through the front windows while the van wound through national parks like the Sequoia National Forest and Bryce Canyon. That landscape was memorable.

Following an extended journey, we reached our destination. Surveying the surroundings, I found them unremarkable. It was a modest, unassuming location, the kind people typically leave, not one they move to. It was an hour's drive and a world away from Austin, the state capital. In contrast to Southern California, the landscapes surrounding our new residence in Killeen, Texas lacked the same allure. We settled with our aunt and uncle in this former farm community now more commonly known as Fort Hood, Texas. Today it has around 150,000 people but I remember it as much smaller, a place without its own identity. The town's rhythms and economy were entirely driven by the nearby military base.

At the time, I did not know what my uncle did, but I saw people salute him as they passed so that gave me an idea that he held a position of considerable importance in the community. I was later told that he was an officer, a captain with his own troop of soldiers following his command.

As a boy, I fancied wearing a uniform like my uncle's, so I was very excited when I participated in the Defense Youth Association league of sports and youth related activities. At my first event, I was given a white shirt and a black marker for scrawling my name and number.

This was my first real uniform.

However, my excitement quickly turned sour. It was during this time that I experienced real prejudice and segregation. It was not based on race, religion, or national origin. It was based on language. The ones that could not speak English were the outcasts. We were excluded from what seemed to be the "normal" group. It felt like I had a disability.

Because of the school calendar, there were a few weeks when both the English speakers and the non-English speakers mixed. I would try to mingle with the others, but with limited success. Everyone who spoke English was playing soccer, but I was never chosen for one of their teams. None of us were. We were only noticed to be mocked. Other than that, the English speakers ignored us.

I realize that this does not seem like an obvious failure. After all, it was not my fault that I did not speak English. Speaking Korean as my first language was not a choice I made for myself. So, there is no one to blame, just a huge problem standing in my way. I felt like I had been handed a very important test where all the questions were written in hieroglyphics. There was no way I could pass! Maybe you remember having a nightmare like that. For me, barely old enough for kindergarten, that was my waking reality.

I hated it. I could keep complaining about my circumstances, but the problem would not go away. So, I took it upon myself to change it.

My early education meant taking classes that today would be called remedial. On the first day of class, I saw a lot of foreign nationals which provided me a bit of relief. I was not alone, after all. But as soon as a bus pulled over at the parking lot, I felt a sense of dread similar to when we boarded the Wiki-Wiki shuttle upon our arrival in Hawaii. It didn't take long after the bus pulled over before they started segregating the students.

Children like me who could not speak English were put into an ESL (English as a Second Language) group while everyone else was sent to "normal" school. From the first day, I wondered why I could not be part of that group. Instead, I was bused to a facility where every subject was geared toward teaching English. The American children my age made fun of me because I rode the "short bus" to school. Those types of insults are offensive and would not go over well today, and it was not any easier then. Squeeze yourself into the tiny shoes of a child so you can imagine how embarrassed I was to be in a special ESL class. It seemed to me that those who did not speak English were treated differently; as if we didn't matter. You either learned to speak the language or you could not join the rest of the population.

From those first moments – not getting picked to play soccer with the children who spoke English, riding a different bus, taking classes with children who were considered slow – I experienced an epiphany. I *would* overcome this.

I made it my number one priority to learn English because I knew it was my ticket to be part of the "normal" world.

Most of the language learning involved putting on headsets and following along as you were taken through a story or asked a series of questions. Tests consisted of English questions like, "Which of these boxes are blue?"

I wanted to advance as quickly as possible, so I made sure to take the tests as often as I could. The problem was that, with the allotted time, I could not take as many tests as I wanted. I did not want to take the remedial classes for three years as recommended. Remember, I was six and to a six-year-old, three years seemed like forever.

Mrs. Sullivan, our English teacher, noticed how hard I was working. She could see that I was doing my very best to move through these lessons as quickly as possible. I remember her saying, "You could play it a little bit faster."

I understood that concept. It was a little like Audible is today, where you could play it at two times regular speed or even four times and finish much faster. So, I accelerated. I not only completed my ESL classes in record time but was speaking English without a trace of an accent within a year.

I have to thank Mrs. Sullivan, God rest her soul, for being an early mentor who took the time to work one-on-one with me. She was a big reason I was able to enunciate and progress through all the courses, encouraging me to try new ways of learning — faster, hard accents and experimenting in conversations with other students. She laid the foundation for my later achievements by taking the role of a mentor who encouraged me to try new things. This, you will see in the latter years, became a call to action.

Additionally, she reminded me of my grandmother who stood as my caretaker back in South Korea. It was probably the reason why I turned to her when I was feeling lonely. Trying to settle into a foreign environment came with so much stress. It didn't help that I was having a hard time with reading, writing and history. Mrs. Sullivan took a chance on me, and I will eternally be grateful for her and her mentorship.

After learning the basics of English, what stays with me after all these years is an unshakable sense of inadequacy, the need to always prove myself. I did not want to be ostracized; I did not want to be ignored. If this is considered an "immigrant mindset," then I am inclined to agree.

If you're a first-generation immigrant in the U.S., the need to achieve, the desire to overcome the biases against people who struggle with English or who don't understand American customs and culture never really goes away. Neither does the persistent feeling of failure which accompanies it. In many ways, those feelings are foundational. They drive much of the behavior I'll be discussing in this book.

The question is, how do you overcome the stigma? This challenge is not exclusive to immigrants but also extends to individuals embarking on a new career path or experiencing a promotion. It's called the imposter syndrome — an internalized fear of being exposed as a "fraud," despite external evidence of competence. When an individual is suffering from this, he or she feels like they don't belong.

English had afforded me a ticket to the world I wanted to be a part of, but the feeling of inadequacy was another hurdle I had to cross over. I was suffering from imposter syndrome. Seeing my daughter, who is 24 years old as of this writing, say the same thing, motivated me to find ways to overcome all of that and prevail.

ACCEPTANCE ARRIVES WHEN YOU DELIVER VALUE

There's a seminal moment for anyone learning a new language. It's when you dream in that once unfamiliar tongue. For me, it was more of a nightmare.

I dreamed of a growling, rumbling sensation in my stomach. I was not sure if I was hungry or had to use the bathroom. In that dream, my family and I were in a restaurant, when I confidently asked the server for directions to the restroom. *In English.*

I awoke feeling very proud. And also, very hungry.

I was hungry a lot back then. I had arrived from a place that was vastly different from the South Korea of today. It was a time when starvation was a very real concern for Koreans on *both* sides of the border. In America, we were far from rich, but food was abundant. My dad was working at a Kmart by then, while my mom was employed by a janitorial service. There was enough money to go around. Our refrigerator was always well stocked. And everything tasted *amazing*.

Suddenly, there was another reason why I was not getting any playing time on the pitch.

During that period, I had not formed any close relationships. In retrospect, it seems I was experiencing depression. There's a common saying about "eating one's feelings," and that's precisely what I did. Food became a source of solace. However, unlike other forms of comfort, the consequences of finding solace in eating are visibly apparent. My weight significantly increased. Even at a young age, I was aware that I needed to make a change. I aspired to become active again and possibly shed some of the weight I had gained. My parents, preoccupied with work, couldn't provide the support I needed. So, I turned to my aunt for assistance, and she eventually signed me up for a youth soccer league through the Defense Youth Association (DYA) at Fort Hood, Texas.

However, upon joining the league, I encountered similar challenges to those I had faced on the playground. It was frustrating. I was finally speaking English every bit as well as they did. But despite all that effort, I was *still* not a starting player. This situation deeply troubled me, and I believe it contributed to an increase in my eating habits. This time around, the reason I was spending more time warming the bench than kicking a ball did not have much to do with my past interactions with the other players or any kind of prejudice. It was not about whether or not I spoke English. It was not about whether or not the other children liked me.

It was size. Pure and simple.

You do not need a deep understanding of the game to grasp the obstacles I had created for myself. Soccer is all about running, with players sprinting across the field for the majority of the game. Successful soccer players typically do not carry an excess of twenty pounds and are not gasping for breath like a heavy-duty engine during play. Perhaps more than any other sport, soccer tends to favor a specific physique, which I did not have.

It's like the world was divided in two. On the one side, I had a collection of athletes who ostracized me by calling me fatso and piggy. On the other side was the wonderful world of food. Choosing sides was not difficult. I kept on overeating.

Then something magical happened.

I was introduced to American football. The football coaches at my school did not have a problem with my weight. Quite the opposite, they were telling me, "We need big guys — at your size you can play offensive line, or defensive line."

Ironically it was when I started playing peewee football and enjoyed the freedom to eat as much as I wanted, that I finally paid attention to what I was consuming. I did not mind being big, but I did not want to be fat. It was too important to be able to move as well as anyone else on the line of scrimmage. Plus, and this really was my saving grace, I was really able to leave my aggression on the field. I visualized every kid that had ever picked on me and transformed them into my opponent. I did not just face an opposing player, I faced everyone who had ever insulted me or hurt me. I stared at them with a warrior's glare and thought, "I'm going to tackle you and beat you into the ground."

It was probably not ideal therapy, but it kept me going. It's nice to claim you do not care what others think, that the only opinion that matters is your own. Except, we all know how successful we feel when we gain someone else's acceptance. I needed to be a better athlete than all those soccer players who had been cruel to me. I knew early in my football career that I would be successful at this.

I soon discovered that being good at football was not enough. I had to be better than my competitors both on and off the field. I had to win at this game of life. This is a way of thinking I share with many immigrants and underdogs. I had told myself, "No matter what the situation, I'm coming for you."

You didn't pick me for soccer? I am coming for you.

You made fun of my weight? I am coming for you.

I carried with me a fair amount of rage from elementary school through my teenage years. I played inside linebacker all the way through high school and have the mashed fingers to prove it. That's what comes from clubbing opposing team members with your hands and trying to rip their faces off.

When not in uniform, I felt significantly more at ease. This tranquility stemmed from a newfound sense of belonging among my peers. I had found acceptance. It did not come from a standout play or a significant victory; it developed when I noticed that my classmates were no longer excluding me but instead treating me as one of their own. I started receiving invitations to participate in other sports, providing opportunities to enhance my skills and enjoy camaraderie. When I ventured into basketball, I was pleasantly surprised to find myself adept on the court. Along with two friends, I confidently proposed a three-on-three match against another group already playing. There was no hesitation or concern about me being on their team. They had observed my performance; they recognized my contribution.

I played three sports and was finally starting on the soccer team in addition to football and basketball. I slimmed down. I was accepted by my teammates because of my skills. I was also accepted by peers who witnessed my successes. I no longer felt like a failure. I felt ready to take on the world.

Failure is an uncomfortable situation. Nobody likes to fail. Failure hurts; rejection hurts. Well-meaning parents wanted to take that pain away and cushion reality for children they felt were too fragile by offering "participation trophies."

Had my parents subscribed to that belief, I wouldn't have become the person I am now. Those early failures on and off the field, in the classroom and on the playground, taught me to double down on my strengths. They taught me to keep going, to find a way to come out on top even though the odds were stacked against me.

I believe that all people should be allowed to fail. In fact, they must be encouraged. Failure is a necessary ingredient for success, a concept I understood clearly from the moment I accelerated my English learning process in order to assimilate more effectively with my classmates.

Without that initial failure, I might never have knuckled under and accomplished the near impossible task of developing English fluency within a single year. Without failing at soccer, I would not have tried football. Without excelling at football, I never would have reapplied myself to soccer and gained a reputation as an athlete in multiple sports.

Having the immigrant mentality became my driving force for confronting and overcoming diverse challenges. If you want to level up, use your setbacks as stepping stones to success, just as I did. Whether you are an immigrant or entering a new organization, celebrate your uniqueness and offer your fresh perspectives. The profound impact of acceptance and integration within a new community or organization can be pivotal in your advancement.

Finally, do not be afraid of failure. Expect it. Learn from it. Use it to fuel your desires and push yourself to take the next step. Success doesn't start with "participation trophies," it starts with skinned knees and short buses.

When I graduated, I was close to six feet tall and weighed 240 pounds. I was a big boy. Earlier, I shared that I struggled with even the *idea* of attending college, never mind selecting one. Ultimately, I opted for West Point, or perhaps more accurately, it chose me. The challenges I had faced until then paled in comparison to the hurdles I was about to encounter, as you'll soon discover in the next chapter.

CHAPTER 2

AMBITIONS TO CHANGE THE WORLD

West Point taught me about how daring to fail often leads to success. Ironically, one of the most challenging lessons about failure had to do with pie. Not the mathematical kind, I'm talking about good old fashioned American apple pie.

Some of my biggest failures during my time at West Point were centered around my inability to follow instructions. This is one reason that instead of gaining the cliched Freshman 15, I probably lost 30 pounds during my first year. Why?

I skipped dessert. As you keep reading, you'll understand why I made such a decision, considering how much I enjoyed food when I was a kid.

The first day at West Point everything hits you the same way a semi-truck with failed brakes hits a brick wall. Before I arrived, people familiar with the academy warned me that "R Day was coming." I had no idea what it was until I arrived. "R Day" was an ironic nickname for Reception Day or the first day of Beast Barracks. It begins the moment you check in and file into the auditorium. This was West Point's version of Freshman Orientation. Except there were not happy get-to-know you songs and skits. Instead, the pervasive emotion was like leaving for an overseas tour of duty as you kissed your loved ones goodbye.

During the departure of our legal guardians, there were tons of tears and whispered reassurances by teenagers promising their elders that everything would be all right. Then the relatives drove away, and everyone thought: "What the hell did I get myself into?"

Well, that's what happens when you have a big ambition to change the world.

GRIT SETS YOU APART

Compared to other institutions of higher learning, military academies are sui generis — unique and one of a kind. I was legally an adult, free to make my own choices — I *chose* to apply to West Point. Looking back, I had no idea what I was in for. None of us did.

Around 50% of the plebes (freshmen) at West Point do not make it to their sophomore (yearling) year. It is a statistic that is drilled into you from the very beginning; one bit of trivia we were expected to know.

If you have ever experienced orientation during your first week of college, you likely dealt with a lot of common anxieties. You had to deal with meeting roommates, along with finding your dorm and classrooms. You also had to cope with being away from home for an extended period of time. For anyone who did not attend boarding school, this may be an unfamiliar, scary feeling. Now imagine going through all of those anxiety-inducing experiences while someone is screaming at you.

At West Point, there were two senior level cadets to every one plebe. You had one of these seniors on your right and another one on your left, yelling simultaneously, "Walk faster, you walk like a chump, you're a slob, a useless maggot."

West Point enforces a hierarchy. There is a set way of doing things. If you deviate from this even slightly, there's almost always an upperclassman or officer ready to put you in your place.

Reception Day is the opening act for Beast Barracks — an intensive, brutal six weeks of basic training. If you ever thought you were cool or a star athlete or just plain smart in high school, those beliefs evaporate overnight. You learn that you do not speak until spoken to. When you are asked a question, you respond with, "Yes, sir," "No, sir," "Sir, I do not know," or "Sir, I do not understand."

That's pretty much all you get to say for an entire year.

No one calls you by your first name. They either call you by your last name, or more likely, a cruel approximation of it. My last name was transformed into a near constant stream of insults and slang words for male genitalia. Your life is reduced to singular purposes: Go to school, understand your tasks and duties, and avoid getting hazed. You are completely broken down in order to be rebuilt over the course of the year.

It's no wonder so many quit in the first year.

Your focus becomes laser-like as you count the days — and even the hours and minutes — to "Recognition Day." That's when people actually recognize you by addressing you by your first name. Until that magical day arrives, you cannot talk in the hallways, and you have to travel with your right shoulder constantly brushing against a wall.

The thing is, by the second, third, and fourth years, the dropout rate is minimal. Only one out of three plebes goes on to graduate, but most of the attrition occurs in year one. So, what separates graduates from the other two-thirds?

That is one of the biggest lessons I learned at West Point and what I hope will be one of the lessons you get from this book. A fair amount has to do with what psychologist Angela Duckworth calls "grit," which I will talk more about in a moment. You recognize from your first moments on campus as a plebe that pretty much everyone you encounter who is not a first-year will challenge you and potentially knock you down. The million-dollar question is, "Are you going to get back up?" If you're called a name, are you going to cower and cry in a corner? In order not to be just part of the statistics, you must get the victim mindset out of your system then get right back on your feet.

Trust me, people who succeed have two important qualities: perseverance *and* patience. You can learn both of these behaviors — they need not be innate or cultivated by your parents. If you are reading this book and you think you lack these qualities, there are ways to develop them.

In Duckworth's book Grit, she asserts that there is a massive difference between Ivy League grads and the ones who earn degrees at military academies. Studying at an elite four-year private university is filled with challenges and obstacles. Yet the grads from military academies are often more successful. Why? Duckworth calls it "grit."

A former middle school teacher, Duckworth discovered that students who tried hardest did the best while the most intelligent students were often not the most successful. As an assistant professor at the University of Pennsylvania, she began researching grit —"sticking with things over the very long term until you master them." As she explains, "the gritty individual approaches achievement as a marathon; his or her advantage is stamina."[6]

Grit is the ability to be resilient and deal with not just adversity but failure. People who become accustomed to getting knocked down over and over but keep coming back with the attitude that, "I can do it again. I can do it again. I can do it again," have the ability to succeed no matter what life throws at them.

Duckworth even devised a "grit" scale — a 12-point test she gave to over 10,000 West Point cadets evaluating their penchant for perseverance. The study revealed how grit is a more significant factor in whether or not someone made it to graduation than brains or brawn. As study co-author Michael Matthews explained, "Challenges have a way of finding us. West Point becomes a kind of laboratory of learning how individuals come to succeed under trying circumstances."[7]

---

6   Hanford, Emily. "Angela Duckworth and the Research on 'Grit.'" American Public Media. August 2012. *https://americanradioworks.publicradio.org/features/tomorrows-college/grit/angela-duckworth-grit.html*

7   Fitz-Gibbon, Jorge. "'Grit' More Important to Success than Brains and Brawn..." New York Post. November 4, 2019. *https://nypost.com/2019/11/04/grit-more-important-to-success-than-brains-and-brawn-west-point-study-finds/*

I arrived at West Point long before Duckworth arrived at her theory of grit. West Point is not shy about pointing out all the benefits to attending but there is also this notion that you are not just receiving a free education. You are also expected to give back because eventually you will be serving in the military. At West Point, it was mission, vision, and values laid out clearly as duty, honor, country because the school was focused on creating leaders — those who endured the worst, including hazing.

THE TWO FACES OF HAZING

Skipping dessert was not for the purpose of maintaining my physique; it was for my own survival, and you'll discover why in a moment.

In sharing what I learned from West Point, it is inevitable to talk about hazing. Some activities appeared justifiable, a standard rite of passage; some went beyond what was acceptable. I will talk primarily about my own experiences, which, in my opinion, shaped me into the kind of person I am today. I cannot talk about hazing without also acknowledging that in some instances, it did more harm than good. More on this later.

The hazing began with breakfast. Students sat around the table based on their seniority. The sophomores are called yearlings, the juniors are called cows, and the seniors are called firsties. When you sit down to eat, you have the table commander, and then you have seniors, juniors, and sophomores.

At the other end of the table are the freshmen. The plebes, the first years, the ones who are assumed to know nothing. It is a fourth-class system for a four-year program and plebes are fourth-class citizens. They serve the others. It is very humbling to ask permission to pour someone a glass of water.

When you arrive at West Point, you are inundated with information. You are not just tested in the classroom. You can be tested at any moment by an upperclassman. Failure to answer correctly could lead to all sorts of punishments or hopefully just a verbal assault. Plebes were expected to memorize everything from the history of West Point to random bits of trivia. And the most surprising bit of information they had to know? The menu.

Plebes poured over pages of menus and pasted them to their doors. They quizzed each other on the evening entree or what they'd be serving for lunch the next Friday. Ironically, the food was not particularly enjoyable. Way back in the 1860s, there was a Senate inquiry into dining conditions at the Military Academy! The report noted that food was "neither nutritious nor wholesome, neither sufficient nor nicely dressed." Cadets complained that "sometimes the meat is almost rotten," often with the noxious addition of some hidden protein: "Bugs will be found in the sugar, and cockroaches in the soup."[8]

There was a breakfast quiche in the morning and a dessert pie in the evening. Back then when only the bread was truly edible, the promise of a home-baked pie must have been a welcome relief. By the time I arrived, they claimed that there

---

8   O'Donnell, Peggy. "The Politics of Pie Cutting at West Point's Mess Hall," *Atlas Obscura*. June 27, 2017. https://www.atlasobscura.com/articles/west-point-mess-hall-pie

had been a slight improvement in the food (at least compared to the 1860s) but it was still nothing to write home about. Yet pie retained its outsized importance, which brings us to the job that we, plebes, dreaded the most — the "Gunner."

The gunner was the poor unfortunate plebe in charge of slicing the pie. It terrified me each time I ended up getting the seat where I was expected to follow instructions on cutting the pie, because that is where the upperclassmen really messed with you.

Let me paint the scene. If you have not visited or attended West Point, you might picture your own college cafeteria. Erase that image from your brain. Have you seen Game of Thrones? Or maybe a Harry Potter movie? That's a good starting place. Because this is an enormous cathedral of a cafeteria, a dining hall that can accommodate over 4,000 cadets at once — all in uniform, all waiting to eat.

Thick columns interrupt the hall's six wings which connect to a central stone pedestal called the "poop deck," while the ceiling seems 100 feet high. Decor is provided by torn flags recovered from actual battles in wars fought across America's centuries. The effect is to make the individual feel small, to feel the sense of awe one experiences looking up at a night sky in the middle of the desert or admiring the ocean at sunset. That sense of smallness is reinforced when you first take a seat at one of the ten-person tables, where meals are served family style and freshman announce each incoming platter of food.

If that was not enough to make us, plebes, feel smaller, the Gunner had to slice a mathematically impossible number of exactly equal slices based on who wanted to eat dessert. The plebes' responsibility was to announce the dessert and ask who among the upperclassmen (and plebes) were interested in having some. Upper class men use this opportunity to unleash their inner geometry. So maybe you need to cut seven slices of pie, or perhaps eleven. Organized freshmen are called squared-away plebes, and the most squared-away plebes carried a literal pie chart stowed within their hats. These charts provided templates for perfect slices and hopefully for table harmony as well.

After placing a piece of bread or a sugar packet in the center of the pie, the plebe removes the template from a Ziplock baggie (meant to keep it sanitary), sets it atop the bread or sugar packet, and then cuts tiny lines matching the lines on the template. Take off the template, and then slice away — delivering a perfect and, what is expected to be, harmonious, uniform, equal set of slices for those that wanted to partake in the dessert.

My temporary posting as Gunner and my attempts to create the perfect slice of pie delivered invaluable lessons on precision and patience. It also provided a healthy dose of failure — at least in the beginning. I also believe it was a good foundation, introducing me to a world of elevated expectations and the elite undergrads capable of outsized achievements.

Now, while pie was the most outrageous and memorable example of the difficulties plebes were put through, there were plenty of others. You were expected to be on time for classes, to perform your duties and keep your living space in order. Failure to perform a duty resulted in punishment of the worst kind. We were required to march across the barracks in full dress uniform for hours. This was in lieu of free time, because of course, you were still expected to attend class and get all your homework done. I spent more than a couple of weekends walking for eight hours a day as punishment for some infraction or another.

Believe it or not, during a 1992 Department of Defense inquiry, pie-cutting rituals were singled out as an example of hazing-type behavior. Before the decade was over, West Point officially eliminated pie-based hazing from the menu. While I do not miss the trauma of the practice, I definitely see its merits — as I will soon explain.

My patience was honed at the military academy. Many universities practically shut down on Fridays. Students schedule classes Monday through Thursday and enjoy a three-day weekend.

Not at West Point. There, you had school Monday through Friday and some Saturdays. Sure, other students enjoyed spring breaks and fall breaks. That's for upperclassmen. Plebes do not leave school. Instead, they take additional classes on military education and history.

But you know deep in your gut that if you can just stick it out, then your time too will come. It's the same with hazing. When it crosses over from professional to unprofessional you think to yourself, "Just wait until Recognition Day."

Back then many of us endured physical punishments that are now outlawed. Some of the worst offenses were even sexually provocative. The most unprofessional hazing resembled what happened in 1990 at the U.S. Naval Academy when a woman was tied to a urinal. She later said: "When I look back at it, I should have cried when they took me in there. I was angry and I was upset. At the time, I told myself that I had two choices: I could cry or just go along with it. And so I went along with it. I begged them to stop. But I was not about to cry in front of a bunch of plebes."[9]

In reflecting upon these times, it's important to acknowledge the complex emotions and outcomes hazing fostered. For some, including myself, the type of hazing I personally experienced was a crucible that taught me valuable lessons in patience and perseverance. However, I would like to emphasize that certain hazing activities, particularly those of a sexual and demeaning nature, must be banned. I believe in empowerment through challenges, but strongly condemn any form of hazing that degrades or exploits, understanding that such experiences often do more harm than good.

That situation says everything about how most of us felt. We never wanted anyone to see us cry, to watch us break down. I hate to say it, but the Naval Academy case is actually pretty illustrative of what went on at most military academies before the 1990s. Hazing was frequent, and it was designed to demean you and make you feel less than human. Some of it was undisciplined, unprofessional, and even dangerous. I am sure there are still people that cross that line even now.

I remember our first Army Navy game. The upperclassmen ordered the male plebes to strip down to their birthday suits. Then we were all handed a camouflage stick. These sticks are designed to glow when you break them and shake them. We

---

[9] Glionna, John M. "Midshipman Recalls Her Rough Seas at Annapolis..." *The Los Angeles Times.* May 23, 1990. https://www.latimes.com/archives/la-xpm-1990-05-23-me-86-story.html

were instructed to use rubber bands to attach them to our male genitalia before running across campus yelling, "Go Army, beat Navy!" Demeaning, yes. Hazing, probably. Camaraderie, maybe.

Is that cruel and unusual punishment? Or is that just stupid? Either way, the plebes who put up with it were counting the days until this sort of weird, inhuman treatment ended — which only happens when a new batch of first years arrives to abuse.

Of course, "activities" like our cross-campus, gameday streaking did serve to unify us — even as we complained about how demeaning it was. That sort of thing is outlawed now but I suspect upperclassmen at West Point get away with way more than people would believe.

Not every "bonding" experience was demeaning. For example, despite being prohibited from leaving the campus, every year plebes managed to go all the way down to Annapolis, Maryland, sneak onto the Naval Academy campus, and steal their mascot. Which meant bringing an agitated goat all the way back to New York.

Today there exists a very fine line between what I consider professional and unprofessional hazing. There is no question that at least part of it is designed to break you down and transform you into a new man or woman. They strip everything away the same way we were stripped down for the Army-Navy game. That takes time. Enduring it takes patience.

Most West Pointers are groomed to be leaders. There are some who dedicate themselves to branches of the military that are more aligned with danger-filled missions. But, regardless of our ultimate military destination, the teachings at West Point were centered around what is moral. Three very important words were drummed into our heads from day one: *duty, honor, country*.

POOR GRADES CAN MAKE THE MAN

Before college, I had never gotten a C minus in my life. I arrived at West Point completely unprepared for the degree of difficulty. My first semester, I scraped by with a 2.7 GPA. I arrived thinking I was a stud when it came to mathematics, physics, and sciences. Then I got to West Point, and I realized, maybe I was not as great as I thought. It was deeply humbling. Also, at the time, a bit troubling.

My ambition and drive were not about identity or family. It was deeply personal, an aspect of myself I only started to recognize in college. As I have mentioned, grades were not a priority for me in high school. Yet I still felt I was smart and gifted in a variety of ways.

College provides a different perspective, one that's both deeply humbling and leveling. I felt talented when I was in high school. But then I joined a cohort of top dogs and suddenly, I found myself in the back of the pack again.

That was my experience. It wasn't everyone's. Some people just have it — regardless of circumstance. One of my West Point roommates, Spencer, now heads a successful nonprofit. I'll admit during the time we were roommates I hated the guy

-- absolutely hated him. I didn't hate him because he was a bad guy or because he did anything wrong.

I hated him because he had a photographic memory.

It took me hours of exhausting, mind numbing reading to get through two chapters. Spencer would breeze through the identical material in 15 minutes. Time management was a struggle for me. The history curriculum alone was around nine credit hours a semester when a typical college class is three or four. It's easy to see that the course load is extraordinary. Along with arduous classroom obligations, you have military training, hazing, and of course eating and sleeping. If you don't navigate all of those successfully, you can wind up with some unpleasant extracurricular activities.

Unlike my former roommate, Spencer, I needed more time to study. However, we were expected to be in bed with our lights off at midnight. As 12:00 a.m. rolled around I was still studying — concealed beneath my blanket with a flashlight trying to extend my reading time. Unfortunately, if an inspector caught a cadet with a light on, they were given "Tours of Duty." That meant walking the parade grounds in full uniform for hours on end.

When you could be studying, watching TV, or getting sleep, you were obligated to dress in your formal parade uniform and head out to campus. There you would spend the next four hours walking back and forth. Rain or shine. And that was for your first infraction. The second one was eight hours. The whole time I was walking with my rifle and my white gloves, I had a nonstop inner monologue of, "Why does life have to suck so much?"

I probably wound up with 16 hours or so that first year. In the beginning, my main challenges were connected to an inability to communicate with others and the related inability to listen and execute. I suspect communication issues might have explained the long string of poor grades that I accumulated during freshman year.

Which brings us back to perseverance and patience. Had I not stuck it out, I would not have had the opportunities my eventual graduation afforded me. Overcoming obstacles by learning from failure is an amazing experience. Being naturally gifted and sailing through life is like getting an inheritance. Learning from failures and meeting life's challenges successfully is like being a self-made millionaire. No matter how gifted you are, eventually life will beat you down. The ones who brush themselves off and get back up are the ones who succeed.

If I had just given up, you would not be reading this book right now, because I would not have made it to Recognition Day.

And on that supremely rewarding day, there were plenty of upperclassmen who tried to sweep the horrors of hazing under the rug. Some plebes refused to shake their hands, because they took the insults so personally. They were not going to give the upperclassmen the benefit of their friendship. Some of them even said this out loud.

The problem is that some of the folks with that attitude did not make it. They did not understand that like many things in life, a military academy is a mental game. It is *designed* to toughen you up. It's *intended* to break you down.

West Point has a lot to teach everyone, not just those interested in a military career. Though you might not want to go through all the hazing and the sleepless nights, I admit that it is the perfect example of the learning-through-failure model.

In the beginning, plebes fail at almost everything. No one actually cares about whether pie slices are perfectly symmetrical, or whether you are up reading past midnight. Those activities are simply created to give newbies multiple opportunities to fail.

Team sports can be a good approximation of the experience, with or without all the hazing. Opening yourself up to a situation where you will fail is a perfect way of overcoming the fear that can paralyze you later in life. Even the best soccer players or professional American football stars fail occasionally. They miss the pass, they drop the ball, they allow the opponent to score. Just like West Point, athletics will teach you skills in an environment that will give you ample opportunities to rise up after falling down.

In the event that you did not participate in sports as a kid, or if you did not have the benefit of boot camp or military service, you can still capitalize on failure-ripe environments to achieve a level of comfort with losing that will toughen you up. You could join a sports team or sign up to learn a foreign language. In each of these situations, you are bound to fail, but you will learn from your failure. You will experience the thrill of getting back up and improving your skills. I highly suggest trying something new later in life so that you can have this valuable experience.

The key is putting yourself voluntarily in unfamiliar situations that require grit and perseverance in the face of mistakes and adversity. Military service offers this, but there are many alternatives that build character by overcoming failure in a constructive environment.

I had a lot of failures that first year but one of my biggest successes is that I finally "got it." I understood its purpose. That realization was a stunning success — one that arrived because I dared to fail. It's also why Recognition Day remains one of my favorite memories from West Point. Of course, the lessons I learned there didn't keep me from failing on my very first military mission — as you will soon see.

HWANGISMS INTRODUCED: LAND THE BOAT

I will now start introducing "Hwangisms" and you will see more of them in the coming pages.

In later years, as I learned from my failures, I developed a series of motivational messages designed to be easily remembered and understood. They are plays on words, or ideas that strike the listener as odd, making them stick in the mind. Communication is such an important concept that anything a leader can do to facilitate it *must* be done. One of the ways I facilitate communication is through these Hwangisms. As I tell my story, I will introduce a few Hwangisms in relevant chapters. Keep in mind that it would be years before I officially rolled these out with the folks under my command.

"Land this boat," is something I often say to encourage my direct reports to finish a job. The play on words is that boats do not "land," they dock; airplanes land. Though I've spoken English since I was very young, I still remember some of the struggles involved with learning a new language. The structure of verbs provides a lot of opportunities for jokes if you can get a little creative.

"Land this boat," I would say to people at the end of a meeting. "Bring it home," is what it means.

The concept is an important one. No one can succeed without their ship coming in. Failure to execute was not one of the things that I dealt with. At West Point I learned how to push beyond my limits and get past the embarrassment of hazing. I discovered that I had grit, and that I was drawn to challenges no matter what the cost. I "landed that boat" by successfully graduating and moving on to my next assignment. But there were many more failures in store for me, starting with one that was as serious as it was disgusting.

CHAPTER 3

THE UGLY TRUTH OF GLORY

Cutting across the desert, nine Apache attack helicopters sped toward the Iraqi border. Flying low in the dark, the aircraft's missiles and rockets pierced the country's crude defenses destroying multiple Iraqi early warning sites nearly a dozen miles away. "Apaches are designed to kill tanks and other armored vehicle targets with Hellfire missiles," mission leader Major General (Ret.) Richard A. Cody explained.[10]

Within four minutes, the Apaches leveled a pair of radar stations and created a ten-mile-long swath of land where attacking planes could safely fly into Iraq. The attack, just before three a.m. on January 17, 1991, was the opening strike for Operation Desert Storm. Over 500,000 American soldiers were sent to Saudi Arabia for Operation Desert Shield to protect against potential Iraqi attacks. This effort transitioned to Operation Desert Storm which gained public backing when diplomatic efforts fell through.

---

10 Robinson Jr., Clarence A. "Gulf War: Apache Raid," *Defense Media Network.* February 2, 2011. *https://www.defensemedianetwork.com/stories/gulf-war-apache-raid/*

The Apache is an American attack helicopter powered by twin turboshafts and equipped with tailwheel-type landing gear. It features nose-mounted sensors that assist in target acquisition and enable night vision. In the beginning, these helicopters were constantly being packed and shipped back and forth from the United States to the Middle East. It was incredibly expensive, inefficient, and time consuming.

A few months after Iraq invaded Kuwait, in September of 1990, the U.S. agreed to sell Saudi Arabia some $20 billion in advanced weapons and technical support — at the time the single largest arms sale in history. The sale would include F-15 fighter planes, Patriot ground-to-air missiles, and Apache anti-tank helicopters along with spare parts, training, and maintenance.

Keep in mind that anyone can buy their own Apache if they have an extra $10-$20 million lying around. What is not readily available is the fire control radar system. Along with the M-1 Abrams tanks, these fire control radar systems operate optic-guided laser missiles that shift the turrets based upon the direction of the gunner's pupils. The best part of the fire control radar system is that it provides a cloaking ability that allows the Apache to evade enemy fire. This was instrumental in ensuring that there were no casualties amongst the crew members.

A few years later, I was in the middle of the desert leading my group of selected soldiers on a mission to prepare a squadron of Apache helicopters for sale to the Saudi military. Once delivered and inspected, they would become the property of Saudi Arabia for the purposes of training. The execution of the asset turnover took several years, all the way through

1996. And during those years, my series of failures reached a catastrophic level; situations appeared normal on the surface, but in reality, were all going south.

REALITY SOMETIMES HAS TEETH

Before I proceed with the rest of the story, I'd like to provide some context about how I ended up being assigned to the Middle East.

Graduates of elite institutions often have outsized expectations. They see themselves conquering the world, running multinational corporations, becoming successful entrepreneurs, or maybe discovering a cancer cure. I was not immune. I had my own personal visions of greatness.

Chances are you went through something similar where your own lofty dreams met cold, hard reality. I have developed a handy equation summarizing those early post-grad years.

$$\text{Success} = \frac{\text{Goals} + \text{Dreams}}{\text{Failure}}$$

I earned a degree in operations research (what's often called systems engineering today). I was also skilled at economics, knew how to maximize investment returns, and had all the training a top military academy could offer. As a West Point grad, I didn't expect that my first job would be the Army's version of supervising a used car dealership. I was tasked with auditing Apache helicopters' fire control radar system in preparation for the multibillion-dollar arms sale to Saudi Arabia. It's not exactly what I dreamed of, but you'll see in a moment that it was largely due to the choices I made.

As a West Point grad, I was a Second Lieutenant — an entry level officer. Everyone gets promoted to First Lieutenant, but not everyone gets promoted to Captain. As a second lieutenant, your first review is important. The Department of Defense uses a forced rating system and unless your rating puts you into the top block, you don't get promoted.

It's not like a job at a private company. You're not getting fired for a low forced rating. Instead, you'll wind up entrenched in an unfulfilling role where you'll stay for as long as you can endure a flat career path. I failed in my first assignment partly because I didn't click with my group. Although by then I spoke several languages, I wasn't able to effectively communicate in any of them.

Like many universities, West Point has a language requirement. I'm not sure if it's my stubborn nature or just not wanting to be typecast as an Asian guy learning Chinese, but I opted for Arabic. I liked the challenge of learning not just a new language but a new system — even if in the beginning everything looked like hieroglyphics. It also took a while to get used to reading right to left and starting at what we would consider the back of the book.

It probably boiled down to a driving need to overcome the back-of-the-pack feeling I'd acquired as a freshman. I wanted to be the alpha dog. I wanted to climb to the top of the heap. So, what could be better than committing myself to an extremely difficult and unfamiliar foreign language course?

There were fewer than fifteen students in my class, making the task even more difficult. There was nowhere to hide. Most West Point professors are either visiting professors on sabbatical from Harvard or some other Ivy League school, or they are top military brass with advanced degrees from places like the Naval War College or the Air Force Institute of Technology. In other words, even if it was just three credit hours for that semester, it felt more like nine. Just like overcoming hazing or getting into West Point in the first place, surviving that basic language course required grit.

Despite the challenges, I made it through, graduating and becoming a military intelligence officer following training at Fort Huachuca, Arizona. My ideal posting was at Camp Casey, South Korea. I had fantasies of reconnecting with my past, learning about my heritage, and maybe finding a long-lost relative. But if I was in any way serious about those fantasies, I would have studied Mandarin. Fluency in Chinese can be beneficial across Asia. Unfortunately, the higher ups knew I had four years of Arabic under my belt. So, their first response was, "We've got a great assignment for you!"

Instead of heading to Korea, I was assigned to a Military Intelligence Battalion which was then deployed to Oman. This meant going to the Middle East during the multinational conflict called Operation Desert Shield and Operation Desert Storm.

THE TIP OF THE SPEAR

Going back to the story of my assignment in the Middle East, our group was tasked with making sure that no United States trade secrets remained on board — an extra bit of oversight courtesy of the Richard Holbrooke arms deal settlement. I was the leader of the team charged with removing sensitive technology from the helicopters before the sale. And the reason we were selling to the Saudis was not exactly cut and dry.

Every Apache deployed in the Middle East was inundated with very fine grain white sand that essentially turned into silly putty when it hit the turbines. That sand could take a helicopter with a lifespan of 10,000 hours and cut it to about 3,000.

That was my first assignment — a combination of watchful overseer and dealer prep. That arms sale deal meant delivering somewhere in the neighborhood of 800 Apaches. In retrospect, doing this was the easiest part of the job. But how do you motivate the soldiers to do the same tedious task over and over and do it well?

The team's job — and mine — involved carefully and thoroughly checking around 15,000 different parts per helicopter. We spread out in a space that resembled a large evidence room. Each check had to be documented and signed off on. The goal was to eliminate the sensitive equipment while maintaining the ability to fly and maneuver. While at the time it felt like I had the project well in hand, I would soon learn that not everyone under my command was on board with the mission's objective.

The environment did not help. My team had been deployed to the middle of nowhere. Many of them were anxious and overwhelmed as we marched toward war. Combine that with living in an extraordinarily monotonous place where soldiers were completely deprived of the normal ways to blow off steam.

The work of prepping the helicopters for sale was initially done by around 30 people. That metastasized quickly. It sometimes felt like an out-of-control cancer, or maybe a hungry beast as the number of workers on the project exploded to nearly 100 — some directly reporting to me along with groups under the supervision of other officers.

I had been failing at motivating the first 30, how was I going to handle more than a hundred?

I never landed on a way to effectively motivate everyone. I didn't connect with the troops initially. I also didn't help them maintain their sanity and moral compass while enduring a desert landscape where there was literally nothing but sand to the front, back, left, and right. It was like working on the moon. *A very hot moon.*

Failing to motivate and help my team maintain moral clarity eventually cascaded into overlooking a problem that could have ended my career before it even started. I failed to achieve a goal that is at once the simplest and hardest of objectives: *Get it right the first time.*

A major issue, which was probably the root cause of the low morale, was that we were doing all of this work for a *foreign* military. There wasn't a lot of love lost between the Saudis and the American troops on the ground. I thought that was the worst issue I had to deal with. Little did I know, it was just the tip of the iceberg. My ultimate failure arrived when one of my men got angry and decided to unleash a torrent of hostility across a very big target.

QUITE LIKE MAYDAY

If you're a leader, you need to do more than just make sure people complete their tasks in a timely fashion. You also need to help them follow a moral compass. I failed because I couldn't get into the heads of the enlisted soldiers performing these repetitive tasks. I should have had more empathy. I should have listened when they expressed frustration and a desire to thwart Saudi interests. We had an Apache that was checked, balanced, and ready to be sold. Unfortunately, one of the soldiers left a surprise package behind. Not to be vulgar, but this story involves human excrement.

Someone under my command was evidently having a bad day. Rather than expressing his disappointment to me with a verbal attack or in a violent way, which in this exempt situation would've been something I could handle better, he opted for a more primal expression of discontent. To put it bluntly: Someone shit inside a helicopter. Maybe it was an exclamatory gesture to the job, the military, myself, or all three. The author got his point across in the worst possible way.

That simple act of vandalism created an article 10 situation — quite like mayday! The real issue was that I didn't catch it. Neither did anyone else in our unit. Instead, the problem was identified by the *buying* party. Saudi representatives opened the cockpit, and the stench of the surprise package was unmistakable.

The person responsible was never caught. We couldn't administer a DNA test, and no one came forward. I bore the brunt of the punishment after word of the incident raced up the chain of command. Military leadership at the Pentagon was informed, and there was a tense diplomatic situation between our two governments.

I was forced to redo all the previous work, scrub down each of the helicopters and personally inspect them before the sale. If anyone under my command knew who had brought the heat, they never said. I hadn't put myself out there as trustworthy, and they all knew the stakes. If we managed to find out who was responsible, that person might face consequences detrimental to his career. The soldiers were only too willing to let me take the blame, and as the commanding officer, I couldn't refuse.

Learning from this particularly offensive situation, I was determined never to be blindsided by employee dissatisfaction again. If I couldn't create an open culture where people felt comfortable letting me know they were upset before stinking up the room, then it was on me.

It comes down to accountability. Everything you do has a downcycle impact. You're not only representing yourself, but you're also representing everyone else in your workgroup.

On a larger scale, the actions of a single soldier can reflect positively or negatively on the entire U.S. military — something we've all seen time and time again from the Mỹ Lai massacre to Abu Ghraib prison all the way to the present day.

My commanding officer told me that this was an absolute failure. It made him look bad and if it looked bad on him, it looked even worse on me. The biggest thing this incident taught me was that successful completion of a job is not *just* about the checklist. If you check every box but you're supervising folks who lack the same moral compass, have a bad attitude, or just don't get along, there will be problems down the line. You can't ignore the signs.

This was my first experience with leadership, and I had failed even more spectacularly than ever imagined. I wasn't on my own any longer. I couldn't focus completely on the task at the expense of the crew. I needed to develop channels of communication that would preempt that kind of juvenile expression before the next disaster.

In the corporate world, you may suffer similar setbacks. It's unlikely that they'll involve bodily secretions, but they might be equally distasteful. If I could step back in time before the Apache helicopter sale, I might pull my troops aside and explain why we were bending over backwards to help Saudi Arabia. I could have provided opportunities for mental and physical health breaks or make the effort to connect with influencers among the enlisted men and women to gauge morale.

Those are some of the same tactics that you can use to bring your team back on board in a domestic situation. A clear explanation coupled with a bit of empathy can go a long way.

But the real moral of the story isn't in the solution, but in the failure itself.

Weathering the storm showed me that I needed to pay more attention to the people under my command. Without that failure, I wouldn't have been able to take the next step in the public sector. And while there were plenty of failures on the horizon, not one would be quite so fragrant.

CHAPTER 4

THE SMARTEST PERSON IN THE ROOM SYNDROME

Lee Iacocca's leadership at Chrysler Corporation showcases how effective problem-solving often requires a hands-on approach. When he became CEO, Chrysler was facing severe financial difficulties. Iacocca, known for his success at Ford, initially brought his tried and tested strategies to the table. However, he quickly realized that Chrysler's issues were complex and needed a deeper understanding. Instead of relying solely on reports and meetings, he connected directly with employees and observed the production processes, gaining insights that were crucial for the company's turnaround.

This direct engagement led Iacocca to identify fundamental issues in Chrysler's product designs and manufacturing methods. His willingness to delve into the operational side of the business was key to implementing strategic changes that steered Chrysler back to success. This approach highlighted the importance of leaders immersing themselves in the actual workings of their organization to uncover and solve *real* problems.

In my transition from West Point, U.S. Army, and to the corporate sector, I encountered a similar situation. However, unlike Iacocca, I was bull-headed. I felt that what I was tasked to do was below my qualifications. Afterall, I worked for military intelligence. It took an electrical jolt (literally) to bring my feet back to earth.

MAKING THE TRANSITION

Before telling the rest of my humbling story, let me take you back a bit. The decision to make the transition was also riddled with dilemmas.

After graduating from West Point and getting my post as a second lieutenant, money was not a primary consideration. My base annual earnings were in the $20,000 region, but most of my living expenses were provided free of charge, so I did not feel a sense of lack. In exchange for the fully funded four-year college education I had received at West Point (along with an annual stipend), I owed the military eight years of my life — five years of active duty and three years in the Army Reserve.

My failed mission in the Middle East, where I served 18 months, did not end my career, but it was a time I do not cherish. I took the lessons with me and tried to forget the rest. After my time there, I was posted to Camp Casey in South Korea for 12 months and then to Fort Meade, Virginia, near Washington D.C. The two and a half years I spent at Fort Meade brought me to the fork in the road faced by every young officer. Should I stay in the military, or should I transition to the private sector?

Employed by military intelligence during the entirety of my tour, I had an in-demand skill set even if certain aspects were not clearly transferable to civilian life.

The Lucas Group, which is now part of Korn Ferry, was one of the top recruiters for military officers. I knew they would leverage my abilities and get me a lucrative job in the private sector — something they had done for nearly 40,000 military officers and non-commissioned professionals.

On the other hand, I also faced intense pressure to re-enlist from the military ranks. One of the perks of being in the military is that they offer you an opportunity to transition into a different specialty. I could go to dental school or medical school; I could be an attorney or earn an MBA. All of this would be provided free of charge.

There was an old line from bank heist movies that goes: "Your money or your life." In some ways, I felt like I would be trading another portion of my life for money. The military benefits equated to two years of service for every year of college they would fund in the civilian world. Between grad school and the commitment, it would consume the next five years and then some. For some, it was easier to just stay in the Army until they earned a pension.

However, my personal life changed dramatically. I was engaged and thinking about having a family. Such thoughts made me less satisfied with my modest salary. Plus, my fiancée was in the private sector. She had a position working with mutual funds — which was far more lucrative than my job. She was a generous person who expected that what was hers would be mine after we married, but I did not want to be supported.

While financial considerations are not my primary motivator, as an immigrant, I naturally place a strong emphasis on stability. So, I made the decision to leave the military and transition into the private sector, which will take us to the story that straightened up the bullheaded man in me.

A NEW PATH

After being recruited by an ex-military officer at Lucas Group, the recruiter told me there was an awesome opportunity at AT&T (American Telephone & Telegraph Company). It would eventually put me at the director level — high up in the corporate hierarchy. Once I was hired, I would have to complete their presidential leadership training program before being placed.

As an interesting piece of trivia, keep in mind that this was a decade or so after the Federal Government and AT&T settled their lawsuit. This prompted the breakup of what was considered one of *the* most powerful monopolies of the past 100 years.

After the January 1982 settlement, AT&T was broken up into "Baby Bells" — seven smaller, regional operating companies. I was to be employed by Bell Atlantic. Ironically, most of those Bell companies are now once again part of AT&T — which, thanks to cellphones, satellite, and cable, is now much larger than it was before the 1982 settlement.

Working at that Baby Bell, my failures led to a shocking outcome (literally).

The presidential leadership training is a rotational process. Trainees are rotated through divisions — customer care, sales, marketing, and corporate administration. My customer care rotation was out of Hayward, California. Part of my job was to understand what employees were doing on a day-to-day basis. The other part was to utilize that knowledge and discover what the company and I could do to enhance efficiency. In other words, I was expected to have a skeptical, even negative outlook because my goal was to discover what the workers were doing wrong. After all, if everyone I encountered was doing everything right, no one would need my insights and I would be out of a job!

I truly believed my education and military background would allow me to enter a room as a trainee and magically improve upon skilled work done by twenty-year employees. Essentially, I was going into the situation assuming that something needed fixing.

Field customer care is union based — "left field labor" is how corporate referred to it. I was in the trenches, working with what was called a 66 punch block. That was a telephone distribution panel that managed a home's incoming phone lines. It was much more complicated than it seemed at first. There were plenty of customer complaints about the time that it took our guys to complete their work. I rolled in thinking I could figure out a solution in half the time it took seasoned electricians to connect the 66 punch blocks, but I was gravely mistaken.

I also learned the hard way that while the crew is doing the installation, electrical current should not be flowing through the panel. In my case, failure preceded the shock. Because I saw my remit as improving workflow, speeding up the process, and maybe even getting rid of "dead weight," I was not aware of what was really going on. That was partly because I was training for a job that prized efficiency. What I did not consider was that sometimes workers are already doing a fine job and the number of team members is optimal.

There was a military strategy developed by the U.S. Air Force Colonel John Boyd that was used to train soldiers on how to make time-sensitive decisions rapidly when information is limited. It was called the OODA loop, which stands for observe, orient, decide, and act. Besides being a strategy used by all branches of the military — especially in combat situations — it has been widely adopted by the business world, similar to how VUCA was adopted from the U.S. Army. That's because the corporate world is as complex as the one the military faces. As an additional bit of trivia, the term "VUCA" originated in the late 1980s and is an acronym that stands for volatility, uncertainty, complexity, and ambiguity. It was first used by the U.S. Army War College to describe the more complex, turbulent, and unpredictable world that emerged after the end of the Cold War. The term gained widespread recognition and has since been adopted in various fields, especially in strategic leadership and business contexts.

Yes, one big commonality between the military and the industrial worlds is their shared love of acronyms! Still, it's worth noting that one of the things OODA teaches is situational awareness. You cannot make good decisions without it, yet I will admit during this time my situational awareness was sorely lacking.

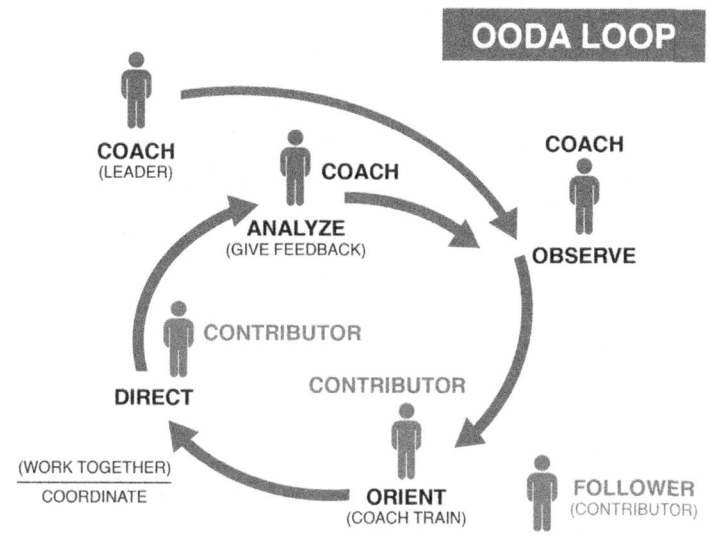

LEARN FROM FAILED ASSUMPTIONS

Most trainees start out believing they are going to change the world. They view long-term workers as anchors — heavy, unwieldy, and impeding forward progress. My issue was similar, though I thought I was the first one to come up with it. Surely, I was the missing link that the company needed to move forward with the times. It never even occurred to me to shut up and listen.

I was focused on how much time seemed to be wasted. First, there was the time spent by the workers getting necessary fiber optic cables and supplies from the truck and storage depots. Then it seemed they were not connecting to the junction box fast enough once we had the appropriate equipment, which meant customers were complaining often about the long duration it took to render a phone operational.

My attitude got me in trouble, because the same employees who were patiently laying the line and connecting it to the homes, eventually said, "If you think you could do it faster, then show us."

I said, "Okay, this is easy, right?"

They gave me a quick tutorial on the advanced engineering necessary to link separate wires and cables to the home box. When they were done, they were required to perform a test to make sure all the equipment was working properly. This was the final step in the installation and a critical junction for customers. It also just happened to be the stage that they were working on when I stuck my foot in the door.

The final test call required sending an electrical circuit from the home to the aggregation box, which traverses through the 66 punch block. A worker (in this case, me) would loop the cable and punch it into the 66 punch block to deliver a unique channel — one per line. Sometimes, there were multiple lines (as might be the case for an apartment building or a duplex), so workers would punch down all the lines. On average, they said there were usually about six different lines to check including backup alarms, internet, and telephone.

The workers I had just insulted by asking them to move faster, allowed me to test the lines that time. I thought I knew everything, and I thought confidently that I could make a positive impact. It did not occur to me that the men I was supervising knew more than I did and had been wiring up so many homes for so long, they had it down to a science.

Instead of telling me that I was out of my league and that they were already moving as fast as they could, they decided to demonstrate.

"Here, you take this, and then punch down on this switch to test the line," one of the electricians showed me.

I moved in to take his place, certain I could handle any task. I was a graduate of West Point. I had learned both English and Arabic in under a year. If anything, I was overqualified for the current job.

Except, every time I completed the circuit and depressed a punch, I got an electric shock. I shook my hand out, startled by the first jolt. My companions kept a straight face, encouraging me to continue. I did the same to the next circuit and received another shock. Instead of coming to my aid, they all burst out laughing. Needless to say, the respect wasn't there.

I saw myself clearly as those workers saw me. Not a rising star or a decorated veteran, I was a bullheaded kid who thought he knew everything. For me it was an exclamation point at the end of the sentence — a perfect example of how the men and women at corporate were so detached from the rest of the company.

They were training me to be the enemy. They sent me into the field with the attitude that the workers had already screwed up and it was my job to fix their mistakes. Yet on one of my first jobs in the private sector, *I* was the one screwing up.

Looking back, there were some important lessons delivered when I was on the receiving end of a current. Number one, do not make any assumptions. Number two, if you are going to change the world, change the world together. Do not assume you can do it alone. Iacocca himself was humble enough to place his feet on the ground where regular employees do the laborious work so he could understand the real problem and therefore come up with a solution. There is a reason God gave us two ears and only one mouth. Whenever it is possible, the best thing to do is to just shut up and listen.

I learned from that failure. Brushing myself off, I ate my humble pie and spent the rest of my time with the installation team learning rather than usurping their process. By the end of my three-month rotation there, we were having actual conversations. In the early days, it was just me asking pointed questions. My assumptions (and corporate's assumptions for that matter), were that it was the workers who were slowing down the process. Instead, it was the antiquated technology — those 66 punch block systems have been obsolete since before the turn of the century. The workers, however, endured.

One of the things I learned from this failure was the value of entering a new experience as a blank slate. Real-world understanding is crucial for effective leadership. It was a lesson in humility and the value of engaging directly with the challenges faced by my team. Leadership demands an understanding of goals, objectives, processes, employees, the company culture, and a host of other variables that are not always obvious. Do not assume that you know the answer before asking the question. And be prepared to learn.

I went into my job at AT&T with the false belief that my education, experience, and training meant that I knew how to connect phone lines. I had never done that before. I simply had an outsized view of my own competency. No matter what room I entered, I felt I was the smartest person in it. My temporary team was only too happy to demonstrate how wrong I really was.

HWANGISM: "REACH AROUND TO THE OTHER SIDE"

A basic Hwangism I developed after this failure was "reach around to the other side." I tell my employees this all the time, cautioning them to avoid the temptation to silo. The more we remain in our separate camps, corporate vs. labor, marketing vs. product development, the less effective we are. No matter what the other side represents or who is in that next room, you've got to reach around to the other side if you want to get anything done. It's amazing how far just listening and appreciating the expertise of other people will get you.

CHAPTER 5

DOLLARS AND DOWNFALL

Every so often, a movie comes out that is so realistic that it seems like the writers had an inside track. Take Boiler Room, a movie that followed a young college dropout's path to millions at a shady investment firm. Jim Young, played by Ben Affleck, gathered all the recruits into a room to show them what the real world was like.

> *"...let me tell you what's required: you are required to work your *1@!* ass off at this firm! We want winners, not 'pikers.' A 'piker' walks at the bell, piker asks 'How much vacation time do you get in the first year?'*
>
> *'Vacation time?!' People come to this firm for one reason: to become filthy rich."*
>
> **Jim Young (Ben Affleck) Boiler Room (2000)**

I've been where Jim Young was, I've been where the hungry broker trainees he was guiding were. I know what it's like to be addicted to one of the most powerful and seductive drugs there is.

It's not heroin. It's not alcohol. It's money.

Think about it. If you're addicted to alcohol or sugary food, someone, somewhere will want to help you. No matter how strung out you are, some part of you will want to help yourself as well. Money is different. We celebrate money addicts, we champion money addicts, and if you're a money addict, it's going to be a lot easier to claim you're a good provider or saving for the future than it would be if your friend found you with a needle in your arm. If you drink too much on the job, you might get fired. Money addicts?

They get promoted. *I got promoted.* Accelerated all the way to where the big boys play.

However, in my relentless pursuit of wealth, I found myself compromising the very morals I once staunchly defended. Reflecting on my time in the Middle East, I vividly remember rebuking a soldier (whose identity we were never able to discover) for a lack of morals over the "putrid" incident in an Apache helicopter. Yet, there I was in my early corporate days, after I left the military, a young adult, consciously making decisions that chipped away at my own integrity.

I was fully aware that these choices were self-serving, a stark contrast to the values I once upheld. This realization, as embarrassing and sobering as it was, has become a crucial part of my story. I share this not just as a personal confession, but as a cautionary tale and a piece of advice to the younger generation. The quest for wealth can sometimes lead us astray, away from our core principles, especially when our mission is misguided by the dazzling but elusive promise of riches.

I had traded the security of a military paycheck for the never-ending turbulence of the private sector. Although AT&T had been broken up as a monopoly, it was rebuilding through mergers and acquisitions. Meanwhile, the Baby Bells were disappearing.

The end of the millennium was fast approaching. For anyone remotely connected to tech there was this incredible energy — like the invisible currents running along a fiber optic cable. I was looking for the next killer app. I was going to get rich on a scale few could even imagine. So was everyone else.

Ironically, the latest innovation came on the heels of a much older invention: the railroad. The Transcontinental Railroad's completion in 1869 opened up the West and made it easier to transport goods to growing communities in places like California. Soon dining cars and comfortable sleepers fed the public's interest as railroads supplanted all other forms of long-distance travel. The U.S. government provided almost 200 million acres to the railroads, feeding an expansion that greatly increased wealth (at least for the owners). By 1900, another four transcontinental railroads had been completed thanks in part to land grants that not only gave railroad owners acres for tracks but allowed them to sell any surplus for a profit. Of course, smaller operations were not so fortunate. They had to actually *convince* smaller landowners to sell rights of way.

Before 1871, there were just 45,000 miles of track across the U.S. In less than three decades, that number would nearly quadruple to 170,000 miles of track!

Despite being a transit mode from another era, the boom years of the late 1990s were also driven by railroads. They became my connection to the fast-moving, fast-money period often called the dot com era.

THE RIGHT OF WAY THAT LED ME ASTRAY

My new focus would be on the lifeblood of the dot com connectivity: fiber optic cable. In early 1998, the Lede family founded Pacific Fiber Link, LLC. The Canadian-based wholesale telecommunications carrier was created to profit off the booming fiber optic telecommunications industry. At the time, this industry was expanding exponentially thanks to the growth in internet and cellular service. However, those industries were as dependent upon equally explosive growth in the fiber optics space.

The problem was, where could we lay thousands of miles of fiber optic cable? We needed to negotiate rights of way. That wasn't easy. Fortunately, the Lede family came up with a novel solution. They negotiated with the Canadian National Railway. The railroad granted them permission to install fiber optic cable along rights of way they already controlled. Not only did this creative solution help them leapfrog over competitors who were unable to lock down such a wide-ranging agreement (it covered tracks across the U.S. as well as the Ledes' native Canada) but the company was extraordinarily inventive.

To speed what could have been a tedious, time-consuming process, Pacific Fiber Link developed the "rail plow." Mounted on a flatbed railcar, the device dug trenches, installed the conduits to house fiber optic cables, and then refilled the trench. Between the rights of way and the rail plow, the company — rebranded as 360networks Inc. in 2000 — left competitors in the dust.

How could I not want to be a part of that?

Even better, they'd hired one of the first people to ever work at Microsoft, Greg Maffei, as CEO. This was instrumental to the company's ability to fundraise nearly two and a half billion dollars.

In other words, I'd been hired by a company planning to circumnavigate the world with fiber optic cables and it was my job to lock down the Canadian National's rights of way. It seemed easy. Yet just as I'd gotten shocked at AT&T by union workers, I was about to get a different sort of jolt from the union workers who had to sign off on the deal.

KNOWING WHEN TO BAIL AND WHEN TO BAIL OUT THE BOAT

It wasn't easy getting all the competing interests to sign off on the deal. Then again, it would have been a lot easier if 360 had a consistent business plan. During my time, I was expected to learn four different business plans in less than eighteen months.

At first, the company wanted to team up with Alcatel who was going to put in half the proceeds. My ambition was huge at this point — I told them I could handle negotiating the rights of way. At the same time, I was thinking that my commission of 1/10 of 1/10 of 1% of a couple billion dollars in revenue could be extraordinary. That didn't even include the stock appreciation of a company that was set to go public in both Toronto and New York.

I was hired as a regional vice president of business development. I originated large development deals. As we shifted from just installing the fiber optic cables to selling a nationwide backbone, the targets started to move. Although the Lede brothers and 360 owned the rights of way and the associated intellectual property, there were still unions to deal with. I guess the moral of the story is when you're chasing the dollar, understand the business plan — because even if you think you have all the cards, a new player can win the pot.

I should have learned that understanding the blue-collar mentality is key to implementing this kind of deal. I certainly respect where the unions were coming from, but this was a boom time which meant that no matter what we did, we couldn't build it fast enough.

And then the business model changed.

Suddenly, my company was spending millions to buy a Montana mine and an entire utility company. As a background, back when coal was king, mining companies laid their own railroad tracks — which meant despite moving away from coal, the Montana utility still had the rights of way.

My focus shifted again. My leadership team told me, "I want you to take the strands of the Montana Power and Light Company — their two strands of dark fiber optics and combine them with the lit fiber strands." I was suddenly tasked with constructing a nationwide, 192-lane superhighway.

I was asked to do real estate swaps and engage in a kind of "Go Fish" type game with neighboring states to get the color strands needed for the project. I asked for one color strand of cable from Oklahoma in order to get other colors between Montana, Wyoming, and North Dakota.

In the world of telecommunications, especially with the utilization of fiber optics, the spectrums of light where communications are aggregated and transported, each lane or channel at the transport level can be defined by a different "color of light." Inside each single mode or multi-mode fiber, the telecommunications equipment from Alcatel, Lucent, Nortel, or others can take a traditional fiber strand and create 192 separate channels or spectrums of light. Today, the spectrums can be further divided into 384 different colors of light or more.

Within 18 months we went from building fiber to swapping fiber, to exchanging colors of light. After a year and a half, we'd settled upon exchanging capacity, and we were finally receiving money.

I swapped a lot of capacity. I was flying from Houston to Portland, Oregon, back and forth. All the while, I did not complain because my goal was to work my butt off and rake in the almighty dollar.

Unfortunately, not only was 360's business plan not sticking but we had so much excess capacity that we were laying people off left and right. My big failure was not understanding that whenever the business plan changed, the scope and objectives also changed. The company was ever evolving and that was okay, I just needed to learn how to maneuver. That adaptability was the difference between staying on my toes or rocking back on my heels. Stay on your heels too long and someone will knock you on your butt.

During this time, I also closed a big deal with Joe Nacchio. He was president/ CEO of US West which became Qwest International. It sounded, at first, like a great deal of success. However, as he was building out Qwest, whenever he had a revenue deficit, he would swap fiber strands and record them as new strands and new revenue. In other words, all he had done was trade comparable items so the company's value wasn't increased but he was making it look like it had. Eventually, law enforcement caught onto his misdeeds. He was sent away on 19 counts of insider trading in 2007 from selling $52 million in stock even though he knew the company was circling the drain.

Around the same time, I was also about to do a deal with a company called Enron Broadband Services. I was interested because they owned one of the energy subsidiaries that became Enron's headquarters, a company called PG&E out of Portland, Oregon.

They were going to democratize all of this bandwidth. I didn't know about the accounting problems at the time until I had a closer look at their business model. One of their tricks was to collect the city business tax they were required to collect but then instead of forwarding it to the government, Enron booked it as revenue.

A few years after all of this went down, in 2006, Portland went after Enron and PG&E for overcharging customers and misusing tax revenue. Portland was home to Enron's last U.S. company. They owned a trading office in downtown Portland where traders were caught on tape joking about "All that money you guys stole from those poor grandmothers in California."[11]

---

11 Garnett, Ley. "Enron's Last Remaining Firm Under Investigation," NPR. February 15, 2006. *https://www.npr.org/templates/story/story.php?storyId=5213518*

I was fortunate because when all of these transactions came to light with Qwest and Enron, I was such a low man on the totem pole that I escaped being subpoenaed. I wasn't legally culpable because I wasn't the executive-in-charge. Despite my position and title at recruitment, I was unable to sign off on anything important, allowing me to navigate away from a historic bullet. This is when I knew that some Holy Spirit was guiding me and had different plans for my life.

I was there when 360 networks went public. I was there when it went from a penny stock to $46. I had almost half-a-million shares — you can do the math. The downside was, I was still in the lock-up period when I couldn't sell.

When I look back on it, we raised a lot of money, but it was raised for a singular purpose. After that purpose changed, all of the committed capital went away. After eighteen months, I said, "Okay, we're changing all the time, what's going on? I have to go do something else."

360networks never materialized. Somehow, by the end of the year its market cap had reached $13 *billion*. Six months later, they missed a debt payment and by the end of June 2002, 360 had filed for bankruptcy.[12]

I was doing deals with the devil because I was chasing the dollar. I had to ask myself who I was representing. All these shady characters I was getting to know ultimately stretched my credibility. My reputation was at stake.

---

12 Mehta, Stephanie N. "Still Afloat In An Ocean Of Doubt," *CNN Money*. November 13, 2000. *https://money.cnn.com/magazines/fortune/fortune_archive/2000/11/13/291579/index.htm*

The bankruptcy of 360networks came and went and so did I.

The thing with money addiction is that the more you gain, the more blindsided you become. You would think what I had seen at 360networks would've brought me back to my senses, reminded me of the morals I once upheld so dearly while serving in the military. But I sank deeper and deeper. My relationship with my family started deteriorating.

Money of the magnitude I was pulling in, especially when you started from humble beginnings, tends to obscure personal ambitions. There was little thought of the future. I also didn't think about how it was affecting my family. There were so many times when I was yelling at my daughter or getting into it with my son. Sometimes my wife and I fought as well. Money changed my perspective. It made me feel like I'd finally arrived, reaching the destination I'd dreamed of during a long and turbulent adolescence. I was above everything other than the score — including petty family squabbles.

By then I was working for EMC, which was focused on data storage and networked storage platforms. It was later acquired by Dell. The company was well known for its very oppressive non-compete agreements. This time, I was actually on track to make money and wouldn't be facing the kind of lockdown agreements that I'd dealt with before. Yet there would be more failures in store, more times when I had to learn the hard way.

A TIME TO PRINT MORE MONEY

During my nearly six years at EMC, the company's stock more than tripled. I was working alongside dozens of paper millionaires, young men (and back then it was mainly men, there weren't too many women at EMC) who often sold their stake and became *actual* millionaires.

EMC was begun in 1979 by a pair of engineers who started out selling office furniture and printed circuit boards. By the time I came onboard, it had shifted to data storage and networked storage platforms. The company was well known for its very oppressive non-compete agreements because they had a culture of protecting their own. It was also featured in *The Wall Street Journal* for its aggressive sales and marketing tactics along with claims by the few women who'd worked there that EMC fostered a frat boy atmosphere.

While tech is often male dominated, at the time of the 2007 article, IBM's sales force was 40% female, and EMC's was only around 13.5%. A number of former saleswomen sued, and the company eventually settled race and gender discrimination suits to the tune of nearly $3 million in 2018 without admitting liability.

It was a macho, aggressive place, which was quite more pronounced when the CEO once delivered a speech at a sales conference wearing boxing gloves. People who couldn't close — "pikers" to quote *Boiler Room* — were let go without preamble.

I didn't pay much attention to its reputation. I was focused on my bank account.

Years earlier, I'd looked at my first paycheck from AT&T. I remember thinking, "Wow, I'm pulling down what a flag officer earns — someone with an O-7 designation (a brigadier general for civilian readers) or more. At AT&T, I was looking at $140,000 a year and thinking, "That's awesome." I was at AT&T for three years. When I left, I was making around 163K. By the time I arrived at EMC, this number grew by multiples.

Before my foot crossed the threshold, the company sent me a check, an advance against future bonuses. Much of my income would be based on how much revenue I generated or how much I sold. Salespeople can go months without a decent sale. Some of them have a tough time staying afloat. While they try to earn a commission, they worry about paying the bills or even eating. EMC's advance was intended as a bit of "walking around money." It was designed to quell my natural anxiety about whether or not I'd be able to cover normal household expenses while waiting for my first deal to close.

That EMC advance check was around $100,000 — almost as much as I'd made in a full year at AT&T! And since I had a team of salespeople, I also got credit for deals I wasn't even in on. In other words, if a member of my team made a sale, I got paid. My first quarter's compensation was $260,000 (of which my $100,000 advance was deducted)!

I was on track to earn a seven-figure income my first year at EMC. Money might not buy happiness, but it bought a good simulation with excitement to boot. Simulated happiness courtesy of my growing wealth allowed me to pretend everything was okay when it really wasn't. The money at EMC sucked me in from day one. My addiction was profound and immediate. I was hooked. My decisions had nothing to do with the long game, with my future, or the future of my family. Every decision was designed to deliver immediate gratification.

Addiction is selfish and self-focused. It's a progressive disease that transforms your loved ones into blurry, pinhole images. Your energy is undivided and exists in service only to you and your next fix.

So many people at EMC were also "stock rich" that it was barely worth keeping count. The stock rich people often became equity rich on the road to being cash rich. That money let them buy seven-figure houses and six-figure cars. The company leveraged its own highly inflated stock to buy a company called VMware.

VMware was a pioneer in cloud computing. When it was purchased by EMC in early 2004 for over $625 million in cash, it was a sterling investment. In 2007 — just before the recession hit — the company sold a chunk of shares at an offer price of thirty bucks a share. By the time the bell rang on the first day, they were worth more than $50 a share!

VMware transformed physical servers by loading them with proprietary software that let each one function like 10 physical servers. In reality, all of the servers were "virtualized" or what we would consider "the cloud." You could actually make each of those virtual partitions act and behave like a physical server. Why is that important? Well, you wouldn't need to buy nearly as much hardware. People usually use less than 20% of a personal computer's capacity. That means you can have five other PCs, in theory, writing on a single piece of hardware.

This led to an immediate change to the approach by the EMC sales force since we needed to sell significantly less physical hardware. We lost some good people over that misunderstanding. It didn't matter to the company or anyone who remained because our goal was to sell the newly acquired software to the clients. Cash continued to flow.

During my five and a half years at EMC, we were printing money regardless of hardware or software. However, the culture continued its spiral of self-centric, "bro" mentality. Even the founder of VMware, President and CEO, Diane Greene, left shortly after the consummation of the EMC acquisition of VMware. That was such a loss for EMC, but EMC didn't miss a step. The printing of money did not stop.

IT GETS WORSE

What do I mean by printing money?

A company reporting 10 to 15% compounded annual growth rates is considered a "buy." That's a stock you want in your portfolio. EMC was growing somewhere between *25 to 40%* on an annual basis. And it did that during my entire five-year tenure. In fact, my group actually sold the largest single transaction ever in the company's history. The innovation that emerged to achieve this feat was essentially a plot to artificially inflate consumer demand. I called it "socially reengineered voicemail." The core consideration was that we wanted customers to consume data storage. The more they wrote, saved, viewed, archived, etc., the more they would buy from us.

EMC was way ahead of its time. There's a reason your iPhone arrives with so little storage. It's so Apple can sell you more cloud-based storage the second you run out. Emails work the same way. In the initial days at EMC, my team and I brainstormed products and solutions that were designed to answer the question, "What consumes the most amount of storage?"

Although we considered emails, after research, we found that these files were "flat" meaning that they could be compressed and saved in a fraction of the surface area of a disk drive. Also, we didn't have the technical prowess to tackle them. Besides, AOL and Yahoo were dominating the space. So, we partnered with the Israeli company, Converse (no relation to the famous sneaker provider), on a product we called Unified Messaging. It was speech to text and text to speech.

Basically, it was a form of front-end voicemail. When you answered a call, it would not only save that voicemail but also translate it into text or take that text and translate it into a voiceover. These audio and eventually video files could not be compressed at the same level as emails (or flat files). Think about it this way: An audio or video file has depth or layers. Each of these layers must be independently compressed and decompressed. It makes the coordination, technology, and compression-"ability" very difficult at best. So, audio and video would be key to creating the demand for more storage.

Such an approach didn't just immediately double the customer's storage needs. No, on average, a customer on the new system would need *ten times* as much storage as on the old system, for which they would also need a faster internet connection through technology called DSL, which they didn't before. Clients were willing to pay us or a partner such as AT&T, Sprint, or any of the internet connectivity providers, for all of it. And AT&T, Sprint, and service providers would buy all of the storage technology from my team at EMC! This is what I mean by printing money!

Where did all this money go? If you ever saw a party scene in a 1980s movie, you would have a good idea. EMC had on file the names of every strip club in the country. The company knew their actual entity name, not their DBA. So, when we lubricated a client's tight wallet with multiple lap dances and expensed it, the charge didn't appear as Scores or Deja Vu Showgirls or Pure Platinum. No, the expense report we sent to EMC accounts payable had an innocuous line item reading JL Steak Incorporated or something similar. (By the way, reliance on exotic dancers to empty client's pockets was one of the things included in the discrimination complaint filed against EMC.)

When I was at EMC, team members were often called on the carpet over their expense reports. That was common at many companies. The difference with EMC was that sales reps weren't punished for spending too *much*. They got dinged for spending too *little*. You were expected to wine and dine clients every night. Weekends were often spent on the links, playing golf at pricey clubs. Is it any wonder my family life suffered?

We had a mandate. We were expected to bring every customer who was going to buy anything to corporate HQ in Hopkinton, Massachusetts. A Boston bedroom community, it was upscale and suburban but it's also where client entertainment was organized — everything from dinners to evening entertainment. We also took clients to Vegas — we had shows with stars like Jay Z, and we had party rooms set up adjacent to the Adult Video awards at the Consumer Electronics Show.

Here's the scary thing. All of this was integrated and expected in the day-to-day culture. I'm not sure if it was used for blackmail or not. But I know that being involved even peripherally with so much debauchery left me with an upset stomach and moral hangovers.

This time my epic fail wasn't a matter of communication nor the inability to quickly immerse in the day-to-day operations. I had compromised my morals when I was at 360networks, but I never learned my lesson. I had to commit the same mistake twice, this time at EMC, in order to wake me up. My moral compass was in a state of complete malfunction. I had fallen headfirst into a love of money and damn all the consequences.

Jim Young's profanity punctuated pitch from *Boiler Room* echoes the colorful language cascading from my lips whenever I reminisce about EMC. The job changed me.

I can't just blame the company. I was a coconspirator, a willing participant in an almost scientific quest to strip away the last traces of my humanity. It was nothing more than a yearslong quest to get filthy, stinking rich.

Money can be a magnifier. Jerks become bigger jerks; benevolent givers become more charitable. Sometimes, it's a seducer, tempting good people to do not so good things. Money also acts like a magnet, spinning the dial of your moral compass, making it harder to find true north and make clear-eyed ethical choices.

JUST IN TIME REDEMPTION

EMC had long been a regular on the *Wall Street Journal*'s front page: above-the-fold and to the right. Except now its appearance had more to do with financial malfeasance than revenue. I was blind and directionally oblivious. That was my failure.

Still, despite its use to soak the customer, I remain proud of overseeing the voicemail project if only for what a technological achievement it represents. Plus, my team was the Supplier of the Year at AT&T which meant the six of us shepherded a deal worth roughly $30 million dollars. Every one of us picked up a seven-figure commission check.

On the flip side, what was I willing to do for all those dollars? Not everything, believe me. I turned down kickbacks from independent resellers who wanted to deliver the purchase orders to AT&T on behalf of EMC. Although I knew of some questionable activities from my direct executives, I kept that information to myself. Of course, I didn't intervene nor stop it either. When you're thirtysomething and you're getting million-dollar annual compensation, your judgement gets clouded.

When you pledge to a fraternity called EMC, you travel on Saturdays and Sundays or any day of the week. You spend holidays in questionable venues including Las Vegas and skip family functions. At the time, I didn't think it was a big deal. Like an addict, I rationalized all of my activities. I was taking care of the family, monetarily. Chasing the almighty dollar means you never stop running, you never give up the hunt. Money never sleeps, it's unrelenting, and you need that constant fix, or the withdrawal becomes overwhelming.

And then, slowly but surely, I started to realize how short life really is and how temporary money's pleasures truly are.

EMC made many of its sales reps millionaires. It also irrevocably altered their lives. On my team, there were probably over a dozen people on their second, if not their third marriages. They lost their way. I came close to losing mine as well — if it wasn't for being driven back from the brink by my wife, I'm not sure what would have happened. She got to me before I completely lost my family.

She remained clear-eyed and clearheaded. To her it was simple. We don't need any more money, so why are you chasing the next dollar while destroying everything that matters? Your daughter is telling you she hates you, and your son won't speak to you. How is any of this worth it? It's the money or the marriage, you can't have both!

Maybe I didn't hit rock bottom. Still, there arrived a moment of clarity, that perfect period in every addict's descent when they recognize the ways their addiction is destroying everyone they love. I started reading the Bible again, and I started spending more time at home and postponing "business" trips.

I started thinking about why I went to West Point in the first place and why I went into AT&T's presidential leadership instead of banking or finance. I wanted to be a leader who made a difference. Instead, I was overseeing a gang of folks who were great salespeople but were also committing adultery and probably a few financial crimes as well. Today, many of them are alone with only their bank balances for company.

My wife put her foot down. EMC wasn't an Enron, but the way we did business left much to be desired. There are people who remain proud of EMC. I think one of the reasons it was acquired by Dell in 2016 is because it lost its way.

My time there might not have seemed like an overt failure. However, if you think about the values I learned at West Point in terms of duty, honor, and country, I lost that — it became all about me and how much money I could make.

I left EMC to accept a job that represented at least a 50% cut in income. Just before I left, I spoke with my VP and then *his* VP and even the EVP. They were all festival buddies from Boston.

It started off with, "You can't leave, what are you going to do when you leave?" Which was followed with, "Be careful, this is a small world."

The implied threat was unmistakable. If I left the company, it would be difficult to get a similar job elsewhere. But I refused to capitulate. I was a newly sober money addict with a supportive family waiting at home and a renewed spirit reading scripture. The conclusion of my meeting with the VPs was adversarial. No one wished me luck in my future endeavors. No one said they were proud of what I'd accomplished. There were no fond reminisces about my half-a-decade's worth of service.

When I was making money for them, they were my friends. As soon as I wanted to make a change that I believed would improve my life, they treated me like the unwanted kid on the pick-up basketball game. It was only ever about the money.

Ultimately, the moral of the story is that EMC was bad for me. Maybe it was financially good, but at the same time, it was slowly flattening my moral compass. I don't count my eventual decision to leave as a failure, but the fact that I didn't leave sooner could have had disastrous consequences.

My family suffered unnecessarily for years while I cavorted with clients and other salespeople who weren't truly my friends. I turned my back on everything important both internally and externally to feed my addiction. The learning came when I finally realized what EMC was doing to my life and took steps to address the issue.

I truly believe it's possible to make money without signing your soul away to the devil. Naive? Maybe. But I would argue that you can line your pockets and empty your soul at the same time. If you want my advice, the failure to stay true to your values is one of the worst slipups that a person can experience. It makes you question your validity as a human being and see yourself in a bad light.

If that happens to you, find the courage to walk away. Read and ingest positivity by reading scripture. Whether you will be putting your retirement or even your mortgage payments on the line, sometimes integrity is worth more. It turned out in my case, that I didn't need to continue along the lucrative path to nowhere. There were new opportunities on the horizon. All I had to do was step out of the glaring sun that EMC and all its festivities created, and I could clearly see the road ahead. It was a leap of faith, not the first and definitely not the last.

I thought that the ends justified the means, and that it wouldn't matter how I got rich, so long as I was sitting on an eight-figure bank account. In hindsight, I cringe more at my behavior during this time than I do remembering the hazing at West Point. At least at West Point, I was a plebe, untested and floundering for direction. Working for EMC, I was a young adult, and I should have known better.

My failure was an inability to measure the toll my actions were taking on me and my family. I narrowly missed being swept up in the Enron scandal, but even that wasn't enough to shock me back onto the straight and narrow.

I forgot everything I learned about integrity and honesty; about open communication and trusting people you work with. I leaned into the party atmosphere so much that I lost my way. It was crazy, and I was riding the wave along with thousands of other young and hungry professionals. But at the end of the day, I felt rotten inside.

Don't ever lose track of your own moral compass. The lessons you learned as a child about sharing and treating people with respect were meant to anchor you firmly throughout life's storms. The chapters on West Point and AT&T should have taught me to value the mission and the men. It was a lowlight in what was otherwise an upward trajectory. The problem was, at the time, all I could see was success.

With the advantage of hindsight, I can draw lessons even from those years of excess. Once I quit, I was determined to set down my obsession and return to normal life. I would stay true to my values, even if they wouldn't catapult me to fame and fortune. There are a lot of unscrupulous and potentially illegal things that people do for money. It took me too long to realize that I didn't want to be among them.

This chapter of my life underscores the vital role of failure in shaping character. As adults, we're prone to mistakes, yet it's through these missteps that we grow. Recognizing and learning from our failures is crucial, not the act of failing itself. Each fall offers a chance to rise with renewed wisdom and integrity. Ultimately, it's our response to these challenges that defines our true character and professional resilience.

Don't sacrifice your reputation and your life's work for the false reward money brings. Though the path may be longer, you can still arrive at a six- or seven-figure income without bending the rules.

CHAPTER 6

THE EAST/WEST CONUNDRUM

Sometimes, our attempt to bring out the best in people yields the opposite result, i.e., it brings out the worst in them. Textbook pep talks cannot cure it. Because no matter how much you think your approach is logical, if it's not producing the result you're looking for, then it's not effective so you have to try a different approach.

East/West is what I call peer-to-peer communications. It is the pushback to a traditional vertical communication process by having managers buy into a concept where the most important communications become horizontal.

If you look at an organizational chart, authority goes up the page. At the bottom are the line workers, the salaried or hourly employees who don't supervise anyone. Then above them are the middle managers then the 2nd level managers, all the way up to the CEO. Those relationships are North/South. When I say East/West, I'm talking about people on the same level communicating with each other. But it doesn't always go as smoothly as you would think.

GOOD MOVE

I left EMC for a division of HP that would ultimately become Hewlett-Packard (HP) Enterprise. I accepted a massive pay cut to join the company because HP's values seemed superior to that of most other tech companies. As just one example, when he wasn't busy running for president, Ross Perot was running a highly successful technology company. A conservative with a strong religious background, he wasn't going to sell to just anyone. He chose to sell EDS (Electronic Data Systems) to HP because their values were in alignment. This acquisition of EDS by HP for nearly $14 billion took my career in an unusual direction.

When I was hired, the current CEO was cleaning up a series of scandals. These included one board member spying on another and the forced departure of CEO Carly Fiorina. Hired in 2005, Mark Hurd's core mandate was a reinvigoration of HP's core values. He exercised extreme ownership — his philosophy was HP is *my* company and it's my way or the highway. He could be a hard man to deal with, as all CEOs can be, but he did a great job organizing the company and shifting its focus toward the growing enterprise market.

I was in an organization directly reporting to Hurd. He was a Baylor man, a Baptist who wanted a renewed focus on following a moral compass. He believed the only way to lead was to be physically present. I couldn't agree more. This was well intentioned in terms of face time with my direct reports.

When I took the job, I relocated to Dallas, Texas where the EDS headquarters were. My wife was happy. However, my physical office was in Pontiac, Michigan near the Silverdome. There was also a second office in Chicago, Illinois near the old Ameritech Hoffman estates area. Along with those two offices, I also had an office in Des Moines, Iowa. Back in the day, Zoom or Microsoft Teams video communications were not commonplace, so I was always on a plane to meet with my direct reports face-to-face. I remember watching *Up in the Air* where George Clooney plays a road warrior on the quest for his millionth frequent flyer mile and feeling deeply connected to his ambition. My mindset was, "I can do this. I'm still young." This was reinforced by a birthday box of Pampers as a pun for being one of HP's youngest VPs.

My first assignment was a group that managed large ecommerce accounts. One of those accounts was Proactiv, one of the largest direct-to-consumer (DTC) acne treatments in the U.S. Although Proactiv was developed by Alchemee (formerly The Proactiv Company), the implementation of its business process was done by EDS even before it was acquired by HP. My division handled the fulfillment and the customer service business process outsourcing operations along with the management of all information technology for Proactiv.

It was my very first vice president/general manager role. At my peak, I had twelve direct reports and six others who didn't really report to me but whose reports were conveyed to me by the Global Business Unit. Plus, I was dealing with around 600 to 800 employees (depending on the season) that reported through multiple layers of management into those original twelve direct reports. It got overwhelming. Because of matrix management, sometimes it felt like a huge cluster of unmanaged, uncontrolled, unorganized chaos. However, I was thrilled to be at a company I'd chosen for its commitment to its values. It was a good move.

EAST CAMP VS WEST CAMP

I shared Hurd's belief in the foundational leadership elements of leading from the front and leading with presence. I still believe this today and attribute part of my success to that reliance on these principles. But unfortunately, it wasn't enough to overcome the concept I introduced earlier: East/West or peer-to-peer communications that didn't work.

I decided that for the health of my business unit, I would rotate these peer workers across divisions, so that each person could experience life in a different department. I reasoned that this move would only help communication and would allow each person to appreciate everyone else's workload.

For example, I would take a San Diego surfer guy managing back-up processes and say, "Hey, now I want you to become the server guy that works together with the new back-up technician from the Mid-West. And hey, you in Chicago developing storage sales? I want you to switch up with Ms. Lone Star and manage the networking team."

My intentions were honorable, but I hadn't thought things through. While I saw East and West along the same horizontal axis, the people beneath me saw North and South. Many of them felt like they were being demoted. They had strong feelings about which departments were prosperous and which led to career advancement. They had houses and families they didn't want to leave behind, and they were reluctant to learn new things after being on one track for most of their adult lives.

When I tried to get a group working together from the East and the West, all these egos and hierarchies kept trying to assert themselves. East/West isn't easy. There's no panacea. Someone will say, "If I have a moat in my kingdom, you can tell me all you want and I'll do everything I can to keep you happy, James." But it doesn't work that way. These siloed departments create conflicts and inefficiencies.

To make matters extra challenging, I had to oversee regional business unit leaders — director level people that hated each other. Why? Because there was cross-selling between territories which meant that if I helped one director, I immediately became the enemy of another. I had conflicts between the high-range server group and the low-end commodity server group. They each would claim the other unit was trying to kill them off.

I asked, "Why don't you join forces for a joint sales call?"

No one was interested. They had become Balkanized, their own East/West standoff and I needed the U.N. to sort everything out. I decided to take all of my direct reports off site in a teambuilding session. It seemed to work. But just as things were starting to click, I got bombarded by another issue and, this time, involving Human Resources (HR).

HP is a big conglomerate. You can't make a change without understanding the Equal Employment Opportunity Commission (EEOC) ramifications. This was my very first time dealing with this. It turned out you couldn't take a 53-year-old guy and shove him into a different work environment and get away with it.

My series of leadership rotations set off so many alarms bells in HR that it sounded like a second Desert Storm. To be honest, I had no idea why anyone would allege discrimination let alone file an EEOC complaint. To my way of thinking, my employees should have been excited to learn new things. If I was a 53-year-old guy running servers, wouldn't it be in my best interest to learn all I could about storage? That way I could diversify and become more knowledgeable.

But the server people saw storage as a terrible department to be in, and the storage people felt *exactly* the same way about the server team. I thought I could just swap them and overcome that ingrained and irrational bias.

The storage guy was young, for example, which meant he was in a non-protected class. The server guy who was older *was* in a protected class. Worse, since he had a negative, preconceived notion about the storage department, his view was, "James just demoted me." For someone over 40, it was perceived through the lens of age discrimination where being transferred into a commodity-based segment didn't feel like an opportunity.

The HR claims started rolling in. How many claims did I deal with, you may ask? Fourteen. Which means the East/West forced conversation through leadership rotation, initially, was a failure.

Trying to get consensus didn't work. Trying to gain understanding didn't work. So, I tried being authoritarian.

Guess what? That didn't work, either — especially in a bigger entity.

I needed to really understand my direct reports and gain their trust before I could do things like enact a leadership rotation. I skipped a couple of very important steps and paid for it dearly. I needed to know my employees as people first. I needed to know their spouse or significant other's name, their middle name, and their interests outside of work. Without that show of interest, I didn't have a chance to garner their honesty or commitment. At best, I might get a superficial, sugar-coated answer.

I also realized how sensitive the rotations were to the long-tenured employees. Change management was at the heart of their fear, anxiety, and anger. For those employees that were 20- to 30-year lifers at HP who were on the previous pension plan, any change was perceived as a threat to their retirement. It was radically different from today's generation where people in the corporate world are focused on their 401Ks. That type of benefit transfers from job-to-job whereas a pension is designed to keep you at one job for life. So, many of the pension people saw my maneuver as an attempt to push them out and put their pensions in jeopardy.

It was an emotional thing. And I still remember to this day one older gentleman, who was probably in his mid-60s, was looking toward retirement when I forced him to move. He pulled me aside one day and said, "You know, I saved you guys during the War."

He didn't know my background and didn't know I was a West Point grad. He didn't know I was ex-military. So, I started with the questions: "Where did you serve? What branch?" etc. But as my questions got more specific and informed, I could see his face going pale. I was asking the sort of things that are only asked by a fellow vet.

I'll admit, I was picking on the guy. I really shouldn't have. I was triggered by the ignorance of his statement about saving me during the war (I assumed Korean War but mathematically, that was still impossible too). Still, I shook his hand and said, "Thank you for your service. Oh, and by the way. I served with the first of the five-o-third, military intelligence battalion and I was a foreign areas officer." His attitude changed instantaneously.

In summary, my attempt to elevate the skill sets of my staff was interpreted as mischief making, and my actions were taken as personal attacks. I needed to appreciate my direct reports enough to take the time to explain my game plan. I could have headed off the entire fiasco with a few quick meetings. Not explaining the shift effectively only cultivated resentment and deprived those who were truly afraid of letting me hear their side of the story.

Bringing out the worst in people is a failure. To bring out the best in people, it is vital to lean in to a holistic, relational approach. I was never anyone's buddy, but I worked a lot harder to get to know them after those fourteen HR complaints. After all, the only thing they wanted was to preserve their pension plans and not be cast aside for younger, cheaper models. As long as they felt safe and secure, I had no problem with how they were working. I assumed I was adding value when in fact, I was just stirring the pot.

IT WAS A GOOD RUN

I spent five change-filled years at HP and loved every minute of it. Unfortunately, in my opinion, some of the board members didn't share Hurd's focus on values. They didn't like the whip cracking and didn't really want any added scrutiny despite the fact that a board scandal had negatively impacted the company prior to Hurd's arrival.

Hurd was fired over an expense report. Yes, an expense report.

Purportedly, Hurd took a female lobbyist/marketing advisor to dinner and was let go because the meal was misrepresented on the report, which to me is crazy. It also proves that some of the board members were worried about Hurd's extra attention. There was something hidden that they didn't want revealed. I can't say what it was, but their lack of due diligence on a billion-dollar acquisition soon after Hurd's firing speaks volumes.

All I can say is that it's insane to fire the CEO of a Fortune 500 company over a flawed line item in an expense report. I'm a CEO today and let me tell you how many times I do my own expense report — zero. I'm lucky if I find a receipt and give it to my administrator in time for month end. My executive admin is my savior. CEOs typically don't get in the middle of this stuff.

Hurd was the reason I came to HP. In our interactions and the way he conducted himself, I saw someone who relied on his moral compass to navigate the treacherous waters of corporate life. In Hurd's place came Léo Apotheker, a German citizen tasked with leading a global technology conglomerate and guiding it smoothly into the 2010s.

As one of his first tasks as CEO, Apotheker acquired Autonomy.

Autonomy was a software business. So, at first glance it seemed like a good play because HP was focused on hardware. The CEO explained, "My overall impression from reading the Annual Report was that Autonomy was a very successful, high-growth, high-margin pure software company." It came out later that reading the Annual Report was a big part of his research. Apotheker relied on others inside HP to do the due diligence. "There were people inside HP who did a good job to keep me informed," he explained and he "didn't have time" to read the quarterlies as "I'm running a $125 billion company."[13]

Maybe Apotheker should have made more time on a multi-billion-dollar purchase. HP spent $11 billion on Autonomy — paying a nearly 80% premium over the share price of around $42 U.S. This acquisition was immediately challenged by European regulators but that wasn't the biggest issue. Instead, there was an almost mind-boggling amount of corporate fraud because HP not only hired Autonomy's CEO, but it came out that Apotheker benefited financially from the acquisition. He wasn't exactly as innocent and non-attentive to the details as he told others.

Just when I thought I'd taken a job that would reorient my moral compass, along came this purchase which was suspect at best. In a few weeks, the media and analyst organizations from every commercial and global bank ripped apart the financials

---

13 Corfield, Garett. "Former HP CEO Léo Apotheker tells court he didn't read Autonomy's latest accounts before fated $11bn buyout," *The Register*. April 1, 2019. *https://www.theregister.com/2019/04/01/leo_apotheker_autonomy_trial/*

of the combined deal and it was obvious that Autonomy was worth a fraction of what HP had paid.

The board had to approve the sale. There were numerous other people involved who must have had an inkling that the company was overvalued. These are bright folks after all. Yet somehow it moved forward. Outside observers who didn't have the same quantity or quality of information as those within HP were right. The play didn't make any sense — unless you looked at it purely from a personal enrichment standpoint. In other words, fraud. I started to wonder, why am I here and what does HP now stand for? These board members that approved the Autonomy deal that enriched Léo Apotheker were the same board members that terminated Mark Hurd over an expense report line item.

In less than a year, HP had to write down some $8 billion of Autonomy's value. Apotheker was fired and Meg Whitman, probably HP's most famous CEO since Hewlett, took his place.

Just like EMC, I tried to run the teams the best that I could, but a faulty moral compass seeped into that subculture. I didn't want to be caught in another issue like that. I learned my lesson. After my personal fails, I took pride in nurturing, coaching, and even hiring very good leaders and team members that were resilient and managed to stay on point throughout the turmoil. I was facing a shift in culture and quite honestly, I was tired. I didn't want to deal with a company that might be more focused on hypocrisy and self-enrichment than on the employees and our customers.

I'd had multiple titles and multiple jobs within HP. I learned a lot. However, after much contemplation and discussion with my family, it was time to move on, time to apply those lessons to a smaller company where I could impact the primary and the sub-cultures.

HWANGISM: EAST/WEST COMMUNICATIONS

The concept of East/West communications is old as time. What makes it a Hwangism is that I've applied it not only to countries or regions in the world, but to departments and individuals within a single company. Everyone immediately recognizes the problems with East/West communication. There's culture and history, there are different work ethics, and competition for the same resources. I want to highlight that East/West is a lateral move — one is not better than the other.

In terms of building better software or creating the next storage solution, cooperation between department heads is incredibly important. As a leader, you don't want your direct reports fighting with each other. They should support each other with the understanding that a rising tide lifts all boats. (That's not a Hwangism, but it could be.)

CHAPTER 7

THE SECRET SAUCE TO EFFECTIVE EXECUTION

"It's a fast-food restaurant that sells burgers."

That's how most people would describe McDonald's. They can't be blamed. On the surface, that simple description seems accurate. So, it might surprise you to learn that McDonald's hasn't been a burger restaurant since long before most of us were born. It *started* as a burger joint. But it evolved when Ray Kroc's ambitions for the business were undone by near crushing failure.

In *The Founder*, Kroc, as played by Michael Keaton, delivers one heck of a life summation:

"Now, I know what you're thinkin'. How the heck does a 52-year-old, over-the-hill milkshake-machine salesman... build a fast-food empire with 16,000 restaurants, in 50 states, in 5 foreign countries... with an annual revenue in the neighborhood of $700,000,000.00? One word... PERSISTENCE. Nothing in this world can take the place of good old persistence. Talent won't. Nothing's more common than unsuccessful men with talent.

Genius won't. Unrecognized genius is practically a cliche. Education won't. Why the world is full of educated fools. Persistence and determination alone are all powerful."[14]

And yet, he failed. Completely. His million-dollar idea was driving him toward the brink of bankruptcy.

The company began as a popular burger shop owned and operated by the McDonald brothers. Kroc saw potential in their business model. He convinced them to let him market it as a franchise. Unfortunately, provisions in the contract he signed left his hands tied. If you know your corporate origin stories or saw the movie, then you know what happened when Kroc met a gentleman by the name of Harry Sonneborn in 1956 — two years after his deal with the siblings.

Before solving the complicated puzzle with a simple but ingenious solution, Sonneborn laid out the challenges Kroc faced:

"So, to summarize, you have a minuscule revenue stream. No cash reserves. And an albatross of a contract that requires you to go through a slow approval process to enact changes if they're approved at all." Kroc noted changes are never approved and agrees that Sonneborn had eloquently covered all the issues. This was verified when he solved the riddle. "You don't seem to realize what business you're in," Sonneborn told him. "You're not in the burger business. *You're in the real estate business.*"[15]

---

14 "*The Founder*: Quotes," *Internet Movie Database*. https://www.imdb.com/title/tt4276820/quotes/?ref_=tt_trv_qu

15 "*The Founder*: Quotes," *Internet Movie Database*. https://www.imdb.com/title/tt4276820/quotes/?ref_=tt_trv_qu

McDonald's was transformed. No longer would Kroc have to wait on a franchisee's search for land and then wait even longer while they built a restaurant and got it operating. Kroc's initial method took too long. The payment of a penny or two a burger was way too little to build a future upon. Following Sonneborn's suggestion, Kroc started locating and buying potential restaurant sites which the franchisee would then lease from his company. The payments started as soon as the contract was signed — not months or even years later when the restaurant was finally opened. The positive cash flow and control over franchisees made Kroc a very rich man. And Sonneborn's idea got McDonald's out of the burger business.

Keep in mind, none of this works if the burgers are subpar or the customer service is inadequate. The only reason Kroc was able to be so demanding was because he offered a superior product at a lower price than competitors. Still, as Sonneborn puts it, "The only reason we sell 15-cent hamburgers is because they are the greatest producer of revenue, from which our tenants can pay us our rent."[16]

The concept of looking beyond the obvious not only applies to business-to-customer relationships. It's applicable in management-employee relationships in terms of knowing exactly what will create high-performing employees. It applies in your career and how to steer it in the right direction.

In the pages that follow, I will share the lessons I learned from the principles that drove the success of McDonald's. It

---

16 Haden, Jeff. "64 Years Ago, Ray Kroc Made a Decision That Completely Transformed McDonald's," *Inc.* November 18, 2020. *https://www.inc.com/jeff-haden/64-years-ago-ray-kroc-made-a-decision-that-completely-transformed-mcdonalds-rest-is-history.html*

has to do with making a drastic career decision and a creative approach to turning around a company riddled by issues from the previous administration.

A NEW DAWN

Things changed after HP. There were some hard lessons learned, lessons revolving like a compass dial around north, south, east, and west. I would leverage these lessons, using my experiences of communications, leadership rotations, and the need to personalize relationships as I started meeting with recruiters.

"Blue chip," they all said. "You want to go blue chip."

That seems obvious, right? I worked at large companies and prospered, so why would I want to go anywhere but up?

"No," I said. "I want to go to a smaller company where I can actually influence the moral compass from top to bottom."

If I couldn't impact the culture of a blue chip company or recalibrate the moral compass, I didn't want to be a part of it. I was done. For me, this was the real way up — a place where my values would not be compromised.

This led to my first stint as a CEO for a technology company.

After talking to dozens of recruiters, I was becoming increasingly dissatisfied — even a little despondent. They kept repeating the same refrain: *Tech space. General manager or vice president role*. I kept telling them I wasn't interested. It was like communicating with a brick wall.

Then one of my recruiters actually delivered exactly what I wanted: Cal Net Technology Group.

As a managed service provider (or "an award-winning MSP" as they said on their website), Cal Net provided everything from data-to-cloud migration to cyber threat protection and 24/7 IT support. I was a general manager at HP. I knew the inner workings of the back office and operations. This wealth of experience prepared me for running a small business from top to bottom. Focused mainly on the Southwest, Cal Net was headquartered out of Los Angeles. This made it incredibly attractive because I had recently invested in a San Diego vacation property.

Besides the geographical advantage, they had roughly 250 employees, which was the ideal number for me. But there was a caveat. They were owned by a private equity (PE) organization, a world I had minimal experience in. Most of my experiences were in the public markets with AT&T, 360networks, EMC, and Hewlett-Packard. Nevertheless, the ability to own the moral compass from top to bottom was motivating.

When the recruiter who offered me Cal Net said, "Let me show you the concept of private equity," my immediate response was, "Private *what*?"

However, as I learned more about what private equity did, I became intrigued. At a fundamental level it was other people's money. It was also highly leveraged. That meant no matter what, I had to execute.

Cal Net Technology Group would deliver what I wanted — the opportunity to finally chart my own course. I was going to be leading a mid-size company. The challenge became: *How do we set expectations at each level?*

And the biggest obstacle from the start? I've never seen morale so low.

I'd been warned. The private equity team that I interviewed with had told me that, "Everyone's kind of going through the motions and not only is their performance lacking but we also are not getting the lift in morale and momentum we need from the salespeople because no one is hitting their quota."

When I started, my initial thought was that maybe the sales quota was too high. That was why no one was achieving it. Keep in mind, this wasn't just a business in the information technology MSP sector –– it was one of the *first* and largest. So, what was the core reason behind its failure to improve morale and achieve sales success? Why couldn't it grow?

No one could give me an answer. My first priority was to find out why it wasn't succeeding. After all, that was why the team hired me. Once again, it was time to look beyond the obvious.

What I soon realized was that the theory didn't match up with experiential wisdom. In other words, what I was experiencing with my boots on the ground was radically different from what was perceived in the Pennsylvania Private Equity boardroom. I needed to make both parties see eye to eye.

Instead of focusing on the theory and trying to apply it, I went the experiential route. Remember, I already had 14 EEOC complaints under my belt from my previous job. Talk about turning a failure into an opportunity! Because I realized, the hard way, how to connect with employees and other managers, I had a unique advantage. With the issues of low morale and change management considerations, it was a similar problem just in a different company. The former leadership lacked connections with their people. They failed to get to know their employees, particularly the salespeople, before expecting them to deliver results. I definitely learned the problems with this from my previous failures.

These disparate elements all indicated that the previous leadership was under a lot of pressure to get the company off the ground. They focused heavily on results and neglected the people side of the equation. But balance is important. People, not just results, must also be a priority; because if they perform well, then it benefits the company's bottom line tremendously.

What really sold me on this challenge was my meeting with the original owner/founder, Zack. Zack was temporarily brought back by the private equity board because the company continued to spiral downwards. Zack was in disbelief and deeply unhappy with the company's morale and the current state of financial performance. He said to me, "Dude, I don't want to do this. PE bought me out and I don't have the patience to clean up someone else's mess. I'm trusting that you can help correct this fiasco!"

SPOT THE BLIND SIDE
Cal Net was beset with challenges. They blew their bank's covenants because they didn't perform financially. As a result, banks once willing to lend with few restrictions were now asking for ownership.

When a company was sold to private equity, the auspices of the transaction were executed as a search fund transaction. A search fund is popular among newly minted MBA graduates who want to fast track their way to C-suite. They acquire a company and become its management, with a plan to raise funds for the company so they can grow it with the intention of making an exit. This means that the former CEO was a recent graduate from one of the finest post graduate institutions of higher learning: Harvard, Stanford, MIT, Yale, etc. The graduate is typically the party that identifies an owner of a small to mid-size business that wants to sell their equity. Private equity financially underwrites the transaction.

Recent MBA graduates from well renowned institutions typically come in with a mindset that may come off as a little over enthusiastic. While the intention can be commendable, that kind of mindset may blindside them from realizing that theory without experience is not sufficient.

Theories learned at a post graduate program, even from ivy league institutions are not a substitute for real world experience. In fact, the lack of emotional intelligence created a negative morale and financial underperformance issue at Cal Net. And it was only getting worse.

The former CEO was used to telling people what to do rather than inspiring them through genuine understanding. Shifting from a consulting role to a leadership role in a 250-person company is difficult in the best of times. It's unrealistic to think that telling other companies how to manage their employees is the same thing as *managing* your own employees.

Despite those challenges, I had the best time interviewing for the CEO role with both the original founder and the private equity group. My personal philosophy is to set expectations up front. I intuitively ask questions designed to help people get unstuck: "What is it that you need? How do you need to overcome it? What are the limitations? What are the do's and the don'ts? And most importantly, how do you believe we define optimal execution?"

After all, execution only happens when everyone knows your expectations.

The key is to start at the very top. I went in with the primary expectation that we needed to improve morale. Improved morale creates less turnover. This translates into better results and a better bottom line.

My number two expectation was that we had to have vision. This wasn't just theory or something I picked up from reading the latest management book. I knew from experience that vision has a lot to do with culture. Since I wanted to push the moral compass closer to something that would align with my newfound resolve, I needed to bring the company together around a shared purpose and vision.

The number three expectation was that Cal Net, like other companies who aspire to grow, needed to hop aboard the acquisition train. Acquiring valuable skills and offerings can lead to a positive feedback loop, an incredible flywheel where each new addition creates added motivation towards achieving the synchronized vision. To do all this, we not only needed to get our vision aligned but we also had to deal with both existing culture and cultural integration.

However, new acquisitions can also *negatively* affect morale. The old CEO didn't help. He was too focused on theory to actually change anything.

With all of these observations and facts associated with low morale and underperformance, I realized that everything I had learned up to that point was needed to reset Cal Net. I couldn't go at it by asking probing questions. I couldn't shake up the leadership team by expecting them to learn about other departments. So, what was the playbook? And how could I make sure everyone was on the same page?

At its core, I needed to make an impact on Cal Net's culture quickly. Ultimately, I wanted to find or build something that was untainted by the rampant greed and corruption I saw in my earlier positions. Moving the dial of a large corporation's moral compass is almost impossible. But at a mid-sized company, it should have been a piece of cake. At least that's what I thought.

To get to where I wanted to go, I worked with each of my newly inherited direct reports and asked them to identify three to five core values that we could build as the foundation for our company. It was important that I not dictate these values. Rather, these core values must come from the managers and individual contributors, if at all possible.

After a week of breakout sessions and managers' meetings, the senior leaders came back and announced that the core values of integrity, excellence, accountability, and teamwork would define Cal Net going forward. Those values were also going to influence who we hired and how we fired. When we promoted, we would do so based on the staffer's adherence to those four core values.

COMMUNICATIONS COMPASS

At HP, I failed in my attempts to help managers communicate East to West. That failure led to my embracing a different process. I fell back on my military training. If I couldn't encourage people to learn about other departments by reassigning them, then maybe I could do it through special project teams. That's what the military does. They bring together team members that specialize in different areas and allow them to operate as a virtual team. I thought that we should be pragmatic in the private sector and use a similar approach.

In any company, there are multiple cultures, multiple generations, and multiple agendas. I read ferociously about methods of tackling these problems, everything from *The Seven Habits of Highly Successful People* to *The Eisenhower Matrix. Traction,* by Gino Wickman is one of my favorites, and he has developed a whole system for maximizing efficiency by infusing culture with values. But what about communications?

At this point in my life, I had been around the block a few times. I failed my way into a decent understanding of the workings of the human mind, and how best to approach people who reported to me. I knew I had to:

A) Treat them with respect and get to know them personally,
B) Listen to their side of the story and empathize,
C) Not assume that I knew the answer before posing the question and
D) Limit making any sweeping changes without first explaining the rationale.

In my new position as the 3rd CEO of Cal Net Technology Group, I was determined to get off on the right foot, and so I developed several methods of packaging information in an easily digestible format which I added up to my list of Hwangisms called Seven Times, Four Different Ways.

HWANGISM: SEVEN TIMES FOUR DIFFERENT WAYS

This Hwangism deals with communication and the mistaken notion that many people have that sending one email out is enough. A better way to get your information across is to repeat it seven times and package it into four different communication methods.

- An in-person meeting
- An email
- A one-on-one
- A social media campaign

All avenues must convey the same direct message to have a better shot at getting through to people while the window of opportunity remains open. It might come across as tedious, even didactic — until everyone on the team starts to repeat that identical message. Then you know it's been heard, understood, acknowledged, and ideally acted upon.

I would tell my leadership, when a person on your staff says, "Really, you said that the *last time*…I got it," that's when you *have* them. We had infographics going in emails. For the very first time, my leadership team was utilizing YouTube. We even had memes. The secret was aiming for ten percent retention by repeating a singular message a minimum of seven times through four different mediums.

This technique was inspired by Gino Wickman's book *Traction*. In it, he offered similar advice centered on repetition and rephrasing. The question arises, if we are already parroting a message, why do we have infographics? Why do we have visuals? Well, those are mediums that facilitate improved retention. When I went through what I consider a management failure, when I failed to communicate, it was because I didn't repeat the message seven times in four different ways.

SUCCEEDING IN SAN BERNARDINO

Few daily diversions affect life in Los Angeles as much as its relentless traffic. It's not just about an eight-to-sixer's miserable commute. It impacts deliveries of all sizes. San Bernardino is the gateway into the manufacturing and transportation industries in East Los Angeles, but just try getting in there at nine in the morning for a client meeting. It's almost impossible. Cal Net central operations is based near the Warner Center in Woodland Hills, California. They also had numerous clients in East LA and San Bernardino that required engineers to be onsite. The demand was obviously challenging. Hence, we needed to open a satellite office.

The ongoing question had been, how could we organically expand the company? The solution was to plant a flagpole in San Bernardino, California. If you look at a map, the distance between Woodland Hills and San Bernardino isn't enormous, except that our client base was fairly wide, including customers in both Santa Barbara and Orange County. San Bernardino was where all our truck stops, logistics, and warehouses were located. We were underrepresented in the Eastern Region but had more than our fair distribution of clients. We had no choice but to open an office and relocate our current employees to this new locale. Otherwise, the commute and the loss of productivity would be damaging for both employees and the company. The challenge, however, was how to get talented, topnotch team members willing to relocate to a place many would consider an isolated outpost?

Being relocated to a less than desirable location *feels* like a demotion. How could we incentivize this choice — and let them know it really was a choice?

Most people living and working in San Bernardino were blue collar. The clients and those living on the west side of LA, especially near the Warner Center in Woodland Hills, were white collar. There was a generational, cultural, and client-centric mismatch.

If you've read this far, you know the challenges I've had integrating blue collar team members into the so-called big picture. Remember the 66 punch block of blue collar, union-based employees at AT&T who gave startling "shocks" to me? I learned my lesson.

To begin the process of opening a satellite location and creating the appropriate environment for integration, I started by recognizing leaders and managers who were willing to help us open an office in San Bernardino. The key was making judicious investments into that leadership team and identifying those that would first volunteer for relocation. We also did all we could to ensure their eastern relocation was as easy as possible.

We provided a generous relocation package. That was a part of the moral compass I wanted to establish within the company's hierarchy. If someone was going to pick their family up and move them to make my life easier, I was going to meet them halfway. A relocation package to move from LA to LA... probably never done before, but as good stewards of culture and motivation, such an empathetic approach to our leaders did not go unnoticed.

I told the leaders that they could do one of two things when it came to the move. They could bring team members with them, or they could hire new members on their own. Anyone relocating to San Bernardino wouldn't just get generous financial incentives, they would also get a certain degree of autonomy — which if you talk to most middle managers is something that money can't buy.

I experienced the best aspects of *teamwork* when we appointed a new San Bernardino general manager. At the time, we had general managers in Costa Mesa, Irvine, Northern LA, and LA. So, the San Bernardino general manager went to the others and asked if they had anyone on their teams willing to work in San Bernardino. The truly awesome thing was that each and every one of them not only offered up possible transfers but said, "I'm going to give you one of my *best* employees."

I made sure that the general managers knew that while it would impact their budget, any team member willing to transfer to San Bernardino was entitled to the identical relocation package as the one we'd provided for the general manager. We pulled in multiple people out of every group, even though it hurt those general managers in those respective areas more because they now had to backfill talent.

It warmed my heart to see that all the general managers were onboard and selflessly giving to aid another team member. They were on the same page in terms of seeing San Bernardino as the gateway into all the manufacturing, fulfillment, warehouse, and retail sectors.

I knew that if the San Bernardino team achieved real results, then the tributary effect for our end-user clients was also going to be outstanding. It would all flow from this new satellite. If they hit their quotas, everyone in the whole company was going to experience some real growth. It wouldn't be limited to one county.

Finally, I had achieved something I had been chasing all along: a company that worked together, that invested time and energy into communications, and prized their corporate values. At no point did I have to intervene and say to one of the general managers, "Give them one or two employees." There was an East/West communication protocol full of respect from one general manager to the next and that included the new satellite location general manager in San Bernardino. They spoke to each other. They worked together. Miracle of miracles.

Not only was there East/West communication, but there was efficient and productive North/South communication as well. The workers who were held up as "the best of the best" were willing to make the transfer because they understood the expectations and they felt supported by the company. We communicated our message of financial incentives and relocation assistance seven times in four different ways. And everyone was on the same page in terms of taking care of the workers so that they would take care of us.

I didn't even have to put it on the agenda in the meetings I hosted because the San Bernardino general manager took it upon himself to visit the other general managers and say, "I want to launch this office, can you help me? Can I rely upon you?"

It was a terrific visualization, the best example of core values, moral compass, and teamwork. North/South/East/West, all of the compass points aligned. Initially, the C-suite was certain that it would take two years to break even once we got San Bernardino up and running. We broke even in nine months.

And then it all fell apart. *That* was the failure. But *that's* a story for the next chapter.

CHAPTER 8

THE FIRST EXECUTIVE (DIS) APPOINTMENT

Guiding a 400-pound boulder around a goat pen in Husafell seems like an incredibly individualistic endeavor. And yet, "There's something ancient and magical about Iceland, and this stone in particular," notes retired Pro Strongman Andy Vincent. "The strongest men that have walked this planet have carried that stone. Of all of my experiences and accomplishments in strength sports, this is one I'm most proud of."[17]

Vincent's connection to a long lineage of rock toting strongmen speaks to more than a unique connection. Even with solitary achievements, we are intrinsically bound to those who preceded us. We celebrate their efforts and memorize their records even as we hope to shatter them.

Because strength competitions took place thousands of years ago, the Icelandic lifting of a stone has its roots in Viking culture. Long before they invaded England, Viking fishermen were subjected to a professional assessment that determined

---

[17] Gill, Michael. "A History of Stone Lifting and Strongman," Barbend. July 20th, 2023. *https://barbend.com/strongman-stone-history/*

their position on a boat. They had to lift a stone. The heavier the stone, the better the pay. Top dogs could lift a stone weighing 340+ pounds to their hips.

From strongmen to singles tennis players, even solo sports have indelible connections to a group. Before a match, competitors carry their own equipment onto the court, regardless of status or wealth. Since many are true global citizens, they often make a conscious choice about which country they will play for.

Companies rely on talented individuals but can't succeed without teamwork. Yet as I began running Cal Net Technology Group, I felt a bit like a strongman struggling to lift an impossibly heavy stone. Truthfully, it doesn't matter how much we can lift as individuals. Massive boulders become lighter as soon as someone else lends a hand. So, as Cal Net faced a monumental expansion, my primary task was motivating my new team to collaborate and move that rock.

WHERE'S THE MONEY GOING?

Cal Net was ultimately valued at nearly 15 times EBITDA (earnings before interest, taxes, depreciation, and amortization); it was a multiple high-flyer, and we were doing great things. Then a midsized private equity group in Boston picked us up and combined us with NexusTek. They had a grand vision that we would become the next platform of choice for MSPs across the country. It made sense because we were arguably one of the largest even before the sale. The combined company was very well capitalized, and we had topnotch individual and middle management across the board.

Then the leadership fell apart.

I had been CEO for Cal Net but now the new board wanted me to become president of the combined organization, NexusTek. They promised that I would become CEO within a fairly short time, however, I was now tasked with integrating my operations with existing leadership and it was challenging, to say the least.

I soon became disillusioned with NexusTek's CEO and CFO. Their core values seemed nonexistent. My first clue that all was not right in this recently created entity was that they would not share financial statements.

As president, I worked directly under the CEO and the CFO. Though they were leaders on paper, it seemed like I was the one running the show or the one being left out when all the players got picked on the playground. Despite my relatively top-level position and my supervision of the entire company, the CFO wouldn't share the financials. He wouldn't share with me, and he wouldn't share with other members of the leadership team until the quarterly board meetings. That stubborn reluctance left me in the dark when it came to a lot of very important decisions.

I was forced to scramble during board meetings when I should have been able to prepare. Worse, I was making serious financial moves without the information I needed to guide my decision-making process.

The CEO of the combined company was around two decades my senior. He'd been in the industry for a very long time. I considered leaving at the buyout but stayed because the board indicated that he would be retiring soon and that I was in line to become CEO.

My attitude was, "Make sure the buyout check clears, and we'll discuss the details later."

It still shocks and frustrates me to this day that I was so effectively shut out from the C-suite. I was president and I was on the board of directors, but I couldn't review preliminary income statements, cash flow statements, or any of the financial statements until they were officially presented.

My previous controller had spoken with the new CFO, and she was in the same boat. She was even seeing discrepancies between what she submitted and some of the final statements. It wasn't a matter of them doing good things or bad things but rather that they were doing things *I didn't know about.*

After the first board meeting, I was pleasantly surprised. The financials looked great. We had plenty of gross profit. We did have numerous non-impacting expenses called "add backs," but nothing too concerning. We had plenty of capital capacity and cash as we began a new era with the combined NexusTek.

We were on a good trajectory, I thought. After my first full quarter as president, the board tried to reassure me that my troubles with the CEO and the CFO were just temporary. Keep in mind, at that point, I had total purview over the entire business. It was actually eight different entities attempting to integrate in a low-cost and seamless manner.

The actions of the CFO had direct consequences not only in terms of the bottom line, but also in terms of product strategy and product alignment. One of the largest components was CyberTrails, a data center company that was acquired just outside of Scottsdale, Arizona. Reviewing their methods, I immediately identified a major problem. CyberTrails was responsible for multi-petabytes of data storage, but it was operating with freeware! Freeware is software that is generally available to any consumer on the internet. Like the old days of Napster, one can just go to tucows.com or a similar website and download it for free. This is not enterprise class, and it is riddled with security concerns for our paying clients. This freeware just happened to be owned by EMC and was released for testing and consumer sentiment collections. This greatly magnified the risk of a breach, a crash, or just corrupted/ unretrievable data. I would always ask myself, if I was the customer, would I want to pay a premium for a service that was controlled by an open community of developers? Absolutely not!

On top of that, as part of Dell's acquisition of EMC, they also signaled to the technology hosting community that the freeware would become obsolete. This meant that most of the freeware would soon disappear. I could see the coming storm and the fact that the company's decisions had put us on the flimsiest of life rafts in the middle of an ocean of change. To move over to servers using premium software, the cost would be enormous. The sort of software you need to run multi petabytes is not chump change. I anticipated an annual cost that could be up to ten million dollars. Because I was kept in the dark about the current financial picture, I didn't even know if we had sufficient cash flow to buy the software and hardware.

Instead of making a necessary, albeit expensive purchase, I got the run around. I made a formal ask and outlined the risks, but the CFO and the CEO were noncommittal. I got "chain of command" and "hurry up and wait." I was still dedicated to the company and its values, and I really wanted to give the new CEO a chance to do the right thing. There was a very serious risk that if we did nothing, everything in the data storage operation would cease to exist.

Best case scenario, I would need about three months to migrate multiple petabytes to another platform. I was told, "Put that into your board presentation and we'll address it." I appreciated the board's involvement, but they were all private equity guys. When I told them, "Hey, we got an issue with this software," their instinctive response was, "How much will it cost?"

Another example of the division between me and the new leadership was in some of the line items themselves. No wonder they didn't want to give me time to digest the information. Whenever I did receive the financial statements, I had a bone to pick with them about their spending habits.

As president, I didn't think we should have been buying season tickets to the Angels and the Dodgers. Only one of the eight companies that had been rolled into NexusTek was treating its staff to those kinds of perks.

Their response was along the lines of, "James, you don't understand. This was what was committed to during the previous acquisition."

I responded with, "We need to be fair, no matter the historic culture of one group. It's not fair for one group to get tickets while everyone else has to buy them. It needs to be one company and one consistent set of core values."

Unfortunately, my bosses didn't believe that a common, fair standard was appropriate. Instead of putting in the work necessary to fully integrate the acquisitions, they just wanted to "go with the flow" and "do no harm!" Unfortunately, that mentality gave one unit the potential to dish out tremendous harm to the other seven business units. Despite my concerns, the CEO instructed the CFO to pay thousands of dollars for season tickets to the California Angels and the Los Angeles Dodgers to benefit one segment of the organization.

Once the front-line units caught wind of this misalignment of benefits, the requests started flooding in. *What about our local teams? Why do I not get perks like those on the West Coast?* The camaraderie began to break down across the company and the CFO and CEO had no clue. It was Nero playing the fiddle as Rome burned. How could I work in an environment that seemed disinterested in core values that it once held so dear? How could I function in a place where my authority was constantly undermined and most of the time, I genuinely felt like they didn't need me around? At that point I told the CEO, "Maybe you can run this better."

These issues eventually became shouting matches inside my Irvine, California office. The CEO said, "James, you're taking this way too personally." I was told to get through the next board meeting, but that I would never receive the financials upfront because they were "eyes only" or "need to know." This lack of transparency and trust created an uneasy feeling in the pit of my stomach. CS Lewis, in his essay *The Abolition of Man*,[18] reminds us that ethics can only be achieved by balancing emotion and logic. But there was no balance for me. I tried to rationalize what was going on but only discovered more questions than answers.

"You're just running operations, you don't have to worry about the financials," the CEO said to me.

This was a defining moment for me. I couldn't pinpoint what was happening, but I was positive that no good was going to come of it. There was no above-board reason for them to be so secretive, despite all their protests to the contrary. We had a major concern with the freeware on the horizon, customer complaints mounting, and multiple cultures to merge with no real progress in that direction.

I approached the board of directors and said, "Look, unless we're transparent, unless we figure out what we're going to actually move forward with, you're sitting on a ticking time bomb."

Needless to say, I didn't get the response I'd hoped for. They doubled down on their promise, saying, "James, can you just wait it out another six-to-twelve months? Because you're going to be the next CEO."

By then it was no longer a matter of my being the CEO or not. I'd seen too much deception, too much waste, and unaccountability. This was not an environment in which I could comfortably remain. I was adamant about the change needed.

---

18 Lewis, C. S. *The Abolition of Man*. INTERACTIVE, 2022.

"We should act now," I told the board. "There's a point where core values meet the execution of what you're trying to accomplish. When you're not transparent, when you don't have integrity, you can't have genuine teamwork. The gross margins reflect our drift away from those intangibles. We need to be accountable in all aspects — from the executive ranks all the way down to the frontline contributors."

This was not about me being CEO. In fact, I handed in my resignation.

One of my good friends and alumni figures at the private equity team called me to say, "James, you have got to take control of this or else you won't have anything left to control." I couldn't agree with him more. I took control by abdicating my role.

This wasn't the AT&T world or the military sector that he remembered. We had frontline workers that were being left behind. If NexusTek failed to support them, they would go somewhere else. We were already bleeding talented workers and spending way too much on recruiting new ones. The long and short of it was I realized this wasn't a good fit for me.

As I left the organization, I personally concluded that this was one of the biggest disappointments in my professional career. It wasn't about the size, depth, or breadth of Cal Net's capabilities. After all, there were approximately seven other companies that were acquired and merged. NexusTek had the capabilities, the people, the market, the capital capacity, the timing, I could continue the list of advantages, but it made no difference. It was a disappointment that leadership, moral compass, and to a certain degree, my patience, could not come together to form a "more perfect union."

In addition to the absence of patience, the reason I failed was that I got sucked into all the drama. I remembered the early days at Cal Net and was desperately flailing around in the new environment, trying to get back to that perfect moral compass long after it dissolved. I thought that by joining NexusTek, I would have an opportunity to guide the vision and values of a growing, national company. While that was true in the short run, I failed to account for the sheer persistence of other people's incompetence. Their incompetence fueled my impatience, and my impatience fueled their incompetence.

The board wouldn't listen to me. The CEO and the CFO were off doing something together. Whether legal or illegal, they clearly wanted to hide it from others. And I thought I could hold it all together like the little boy with his finger stuck in the dam. I had to take my elevated hopes and dreams elsewhere.

EXECUTION IS EVERYTHING

In competition, you might have ten brawny guys versus ten puny guys. Appearances can be deceiving. If the larger competitors are overconfident or just a collection of individual strongmen, their victory is far from guaranteed. The slighter competitors may be better trained. They may be a more cohesive unit. They may be the winners.

Also, an individual's ability to get results might actually be counterproductive if they are heading in a different direction from everyone else. A strongest man competition is about the individual, but a cohesive group can outmatch the mightiest of strongmen.

Consider the showdown between the LA Lakers and the Portland Trail Blazers in 2000. The Lakers had Shaq, Kobe Bryant, and Rick Fox, whereas Portland leaned heavily on its one and only star, Scottie Pippin. The Lakers were able to work as a team, outperforming the Trail Blazers and cementing their dominance in the region.

My personal philosophy has always been that it's okay if your department appears to be a motley collection of disparate individuals. It's okay if one person outshines another. You just have to trust that both the star performer and those that are weak performers will be willing to do their jobs, even when no one is watching. Furthermore, teammates, regardless of capability, might even do a bit of ad hoc coaching directed toward anyone who needs it. That's what being on a team is about — you're not hoping someone stumbles so you can save the day. You aren't celebrating another's failure. Instead, you're helping them become successful. Ultimately, you need to *trust*.

Recognize that if you maintain open communication networks, others will let you know if they need help. They will also help others be a part of the team.

Gino Wickman talks about recruiting people that understand where you're going and have the desire to obtain that milestone with you. Just as significant, they must have the capacity to learn and execute to help you reach your destination. In short, "they get it, they want it, they have the capacity to do it."[19] I would add that each member must also be able to participate in the camaraderie to make the overall team become better. This allows the group to meet any challenges and overcome any obstacles.

---

19 Wickman, Gino. *Traction*. 2012. BenBella Books

When you have integrity, excellence, accountability, and teamwork, then it's no longer my silo versus your silo. Instead, it becomes an intertwined, interconnected team. This is what I had hoped to achieve my first time running a company, and for a while, it seemed to come true. Unfortunately, the deck shifted in mid play, and what I thought was a winning hand lost out.

It was time to walk away. I failed to execute the potential and convert it to reality. We had all the advantages but could not win. I was prepared to take all these lessons learned and apply them to something more personal. I was going to invest in something for me.

CHAPTER 9

CARS AND COMING OF AGE

A short, few months after I vacated my role at NexusTek, I heard that the private equity team took my advice and terminated both the CEO and CFO at the same time. As I understood it, the reason for the CEO and CFO terminations was for "accounting irregularities" and "lack of team cohesion." Duh! Nevertheless, after multiple failures in business and a distinct lack of values, I decided to move from corporate America and try my own thing. I have always loved cars, so I reasoned that I could easily sell them. I had enough money saved up from multiple ventures to invest in something I would love to do.

My wife said to me once, "I don't know why you're pushing so hard. We are so fortunate and doing fine. Just let the NexusTek thing go."

I took her advice and decided to pursue a passion project. I figured that it would be easy to establish a company culture if I was the founder and CEO. I would use what I learned from my previous positions and improve upon it. I proposed that I would create an honest car dealership, connecting people like me to sweet rides. I wanted to make sure that the company provided experiences both to our clients and our employees with integrity and core values that I felt was lacking in some of the other companies with whom I was once associated. I also thought that I could add a moral compass to the automotive distribution industry which has notoriously been given a black eye for the perceptions of its lack of core values.

As I became more excited at the thought of creating my venture, I thought to myself that I wouldn't have to deal with any entrenched culture or people who had outlived their usefulness. I would be starting fresh, and I would make my business one for the record books. It was the same aspiration as any dreamer or entrepreneur. But it was another example of me diving in headfirst into a situation thinking that I could change the world (or at least the workgroup) before getting my bearings. I would soon learn firsthand that the underlying sub-cultures of automobile distributorships were deeply entrenched. No matter how much I wanted my company to be different, I was swimming upstream without a paddle.

My failure this time around was a lack of appreciation for industry veterans, and the lengths they would go to for a sale.

It all started with my own vehicles. As I mentioned, I loved cars. It was always a kind of hobby with me. I have had the opportunity to ride or even buy mainstream sports cars, popular sports utility vehicles, jeeps, trucks, and even luxury convertibles...name the type and model of a mainstream car, and I have either driven the vehicle or bought it, depreciated it, and resold it. I didn't smoke, drink, or have any weird idiosyncrasies. What vice I did have was a borderline addiction to cars!

As part of that passion, going into business in the automotive industry was now my focus. I decided that such a business would be a perfect way to combine my interests in cars and culture (not to mention save some personal expenses in buying and selling my own vehicles). I envisioned myself talking shop to customers, selling them on the best investment for their midlife crisis. I invested in a used car dealership that primarily sold exotic, sports, and luxury cars. Little did I know, but it is probably the most expensive venture that you can get yourself into. And if you want to talk about moral compass, it's probably also the most nascent.

It cost me close to $5 million that I could have reinvested back into the family. Without a regular 9-5, I could have been spending that time paying attention to my kids and my wife, doing all the things that I needed to do as a husband and father. But I didn't. That's a topic for a later chapter, but for now, I'll just say that I was determined to throw myself back into the ring.

I wanted to make money, but I also wanted to create something good. Unfortunately, the car dealership did neither. I actually lost money, and the company was dragged down along with many other small dealerships, due to a lack of moral compass.

LOOK BEFORE YOU LEAP

Following a passion is one thing, but you have to listen to your gut. My gut was telling me that something was off, but I continued to pour more money in. By the time I realized that my salesmen were shady, and that the entire business was a sham, it was too late.

The people that I picked up grew up in a life where it was normal to inflate prices. They were only concerned with what they could get away with. It wasn't a matter of integrity, but just a matter of not getting caught. If no one found out, they were just as happy to keep fleecing the customer, ripping me off and laughing all the way to the bank. No offense to those that have created an honest living in the automotive industry. Unfortunately, in my short-lived experience, I just didn't come across too many representatives in the areas of automotive sales, manufacturing, financing, trading, or even transportation that had many scruples. Corruption within the group that I designed was rampant.

Back in the days when a GCR Dodge Viper V 10 engine came out, one of the original Roadsters would retail for typically $100,000. A respectable markup currently would put the purchase price at around $120,000, but that wasn't good enough for my salespeople. They wanted to have a dealer delivery charge, leasing paperwork charge, and every other fee they could think of. They just kept piling on the additions until pretty soon, the customer was paying upwards of $130,000. It was greed, pure and simple.

These salespeople were trying to widen the gap. They intended to nickel and dime the customer from a $90,000 acquisition price to a sales price of $130,000 or more. What was called the "dealer pack" should have been better stated as the "salesman's fat."

The managers didn't even care if it ever got sold. It was all about the markup, not the sale, and the difference was something I was expected to cover. For example, let's say that there was a trade-in of an older vehicle. The trade-in credit may have been $10,000 but on paper, they would represent that to the dealership as $5,000. How could they get away with this? Because on paper, they were making the dealership lots of money. In actuality, the credit given to the client and the actual depreciation of the vehicle sitting on the lot were two different things. The manager and the sales representatives didn't care about the company winning. They only cared about the individual transaction and how *they* could win. Every day a car sat on the lot, there was a daily holding inventory cost. So, if you traded a vehicle and the customer bought another car, great. But every day a $10,000 trade-in sat on the lot, the cost to sell it would increase. Moreover, the traded-in vehicle loses value the longer it sits, and the costs associated with prepping the vehicle for resale or auction were not taken into account.

By the time I learned the ugly lessons of the automotive dealership, I was in deep. The trade-in inventory grew out of control, the asset values were too inflated, and the cost of the inventory to prepare for resale was woefully underestimated. Yet, at the transaction level, every customer deal was profitable. Unfortunately, it was far from reality. Dollars flew out of my pocket, and into the pockets of the dubious salespeople and the demanding banking institutions.

CORRUPTION COMES STANDARD

If there is a silver-lining, it was that I got to drive every car under the sun. I had all the Hummers that you could ever want, and when Vipers or Corvettes were hot, I could get you one. I had Ferraris of various makes and models, but I was hemorrhaging cash.

Because we had a dealer's tag, we never had to pay taxes for cars that we drove. I could go to any dealership and say, "Hey, can I borrow that?" A new car dealership doesn't care if a used car dealership comes in and goes, "I want to sell that, I have a client for you." Instead of arguing, they will say, "Great, here's my price."

It was a money driven culture. And because cars are flashy and exciting, it attracted a lot of passionate investors, like myself. But as I would soon come to realize, we were just a bunch of misguided investors masquerading as car aficionados.

I was one of those. And the more energy I put into the dealership, the less I had left for my family. I had a horrible work-life balance. I kept trying to figure out what was going wrong while my staff was undermining my authority at every turn.

I got to know everything about dealer packs, leasing, rate factors, and how you can infiltrate the bank's indirect lenders. If you think about it, not many people pay cash for a car. That's why indirect lending is so critical. We were handing customers off to banks for bad loans and kickbacks. There was no concern for anything other than the almighty dollar.

Subsequently, I lost $5 million off that investment. I had to file for corporate bankruptcy. I gave my direct hires the run of the place and expected them to act honestly. But they were only looking out for their best interest. And who could blame them? They were just playing by the rules of the game; I was the one who didn't study the playbook — which I didn't want to abide by.

CASINO ETHICS

If you want to run a car dealership, someone's got to watch you and someone else has to watch them and someone else has got to watch the watchers. You can never leave anyone alone on a sales call or in a meeting with the loan officers. It was like a casino mentality, where the best way to operate is just to assume that everyone is corrupt.

An old friend of mine worked in a call center for a dealership and it aged her. She suffered constantly working with self-centered people. There was so much corruption, it felt like I was in bed with the mafia.

The depreciation cycle of cars is one of the biggest tax havens ever. The dealership takes ownership of the car and pays for it with a credit line. They borrow for a day, but the next day, the bank says, "I want the money." So, the car just gets transferred from one dealership to the next, from your credit line to someone else's.

Accelerated tax depreciation for all vehicles is the biggest scam in the world. People that don't have cash can make tons of money. At first, I was like, "Oh, man, this is awesome." But in the end, when I realized that I was the sucker, I had to get out of it.

For me, it was a bad business model. I didn't want to become profitable at the expense of my clients. I didn't have the wherewithal or the interest in continuing once I realized what was happening. There were too many moving parts, and too much of the energy was going into perpetuating the game, doing an end run around the banks, and juggling inventory.

My failure in this venture was my ego. I thought I was too experienced to fail. I thought I had seen everything and that by owning the business, I could chart its course. If you're reading this to learn from my failures, the takeaway would be to remove your rose-colored glasses. Don't let emotion blind you. Learn the business then try to earn. There are no shortcuts.

I was like some kind of dreamy, fourth-grade kid, skipping down the primrose path, paying no attention to my surroundings. *Cars*, I thought. How could I go wrong? It was yet another example of putting the cart before the horse. I had no idea what the culture was in the industry I bought into, and it cost me dearly.

If I could have leveraged the lessons learned in the previous chapters, as opposed to jumping in with both feet thinking that my leadership experience would transfer from one situation to the next, I would have been in a much better position.

Everyone was still after the almighty dollar, even more so in some respects. I consider myself a good guy, but I made a deal with the devil.

Part of my failure was the inability to hold anyone accountable for the trades. Trade ins were undervalued or overvalued, depending on how each salesperson wanted to handle it. There was no process of checks and balances. I was forced to rely on people who I would later discover were scamming everyone left and right. Ultimately, I take full responsibility.

I should have looked before I leapt and made an educated decision as to whether I wanted to get into auto sales.

It didn't take me long to realize my mistake. This was failure in the blink of an eye. It was a good lesson learned, but the world didn't stop there. At the same time, I was failing in the car auction, I was failing much closer to home. My family situation was getting tense, and it all came down to a lack of attention on my part.

This is the worst place to fail, as some of you may be aware. Jobs you can walk away from, industries you can leave, but your family should be forever. I got on my high horse about making money and didn't notice I was hurting my children in the process. If you read any segment with care, I hope it's the next one. Leadership isn't just important in the boardroom or on the showroom floor, it also hits closer to home.

FAMILY FAILS

Around the time I was focusing (and failing) on the car business, my children were coming of age with still so much to learn, yet I was the one being schooled at life, at being a parent. I was, once again, failing, but I was also learning...massively.

"I can't believe you lost! Are you kidding me?!" I shouted, turning away from the child standing on the tennis court.

As a father, I didn't have the best role models growing up, and I royally screwed up every single thing that I could have screwed up. I watched my daughter, a finalist in one of the most prestigious tennis tournaments in the country, get beaten by an opponent I knew was weaker. And what did I do? I didn't console her or tell her how proud I was of her. I didn't suggest that she move forward and focus on the next match and learn from her loss. No, I shouted at her. I failed so miserably!

My daughter, Madison, won the Texas Grand Slam Tennis Tournament for girls' singles, and she was a finalist for doubles at the 12- and 14-year-old divisions. I remember her exhilaration and the emotional high when she competed in these tournaments. At the Nationals tournaments, it was heartbreaking to see her lose in the late rounds, especially in matches that she could have won. During those days of failure, I didn't even hear what I was saying. I wanted her to win, and I lashed out when she didn't.

At one Nationals tournament in California, I remember watching another parent berating their child for losing. I caught the eye of the player and at that instant, I saw my daughter mirrored back to me. I finally realized what it sounded like to my child. The guilt that washed over me was intense, and I could not stop crying.

It was like a jolt to my heart. I saw what we were doing to my own flesh and blood and how she really just needed some space and some support. I was not empathetic. I was cruel. I was not a leader. I was an instigator. I was emotional and had no discernment.

As a leader, you can't let your emotions get the best of you. When someone screws up, you have a choice to make. And when your family is involved, the choice is clear. You help your child learn from their mistakes and focus on the things under their control. I did this better in my workplace than I did at home. When I was emotional, I lost my ability to be empathetic and even compassionate. It took another parent mistreating their child to make me really see what I was doing.

Neither my daughter nor this other unlucky child was trying to lose. Maybe they had a bad game, maybe they didn't get enough sleep or maybe the sun was in their eyes. Whatever the reason for the inability to execute, we weren't going to accomplish anything by minimizing their effort. If the goal was to do better next time, to win a national tournament then insulting words had no place in the conversation.

LEADERSHIP IS ALL AROUND YOU

Everything that I knew about leadership went right out the door when I was dealing with my own family. I was a West Point graduate; I'd been CEO and owner of my own business. I read the Bible and thought I was a good Christian. But none of my past deeds seemed to translate into the leadership skills necessary to comfort and nurture my own family. To my children, both Madison and Colby, who will someday read this book, I will forever be apologetic and ask for their continual forgiveness. It should not have taken another failed parent to allow me to come to my senses.

You can't motivate anyone by yelling at them. That was managerial skills 101 and something I learned as a plebe at West Point. All that time I spent dodging the hazing rituals hadn't taught me a thing when it came to my own family. I thought back to the guys who wouldn't look the upperclassmen in the eye after recognition day. It was wrong then, and I didn't even care about those guys.

I understand that family leadership can be tricky because there are emotions involved. Of course, anyone who tells you to check your baggage at the office door is dreaming. People bring all kinds of nonsense to the table no matter what the stakes.

Case in point, at the auto dealership, the people I hired were bringing with them the experience they had at the last place. They were playing a game I wasn't aware of, until it finally came back to bite me in the butt.

With loved ones, it can be even more difficult to separate process from emotion. Kids don't have experience with communication and teamwork. The family is their first environment and if you're not providing guidance the way you should, it can be a disaster.

My wife and I have one daughter and one son. They are both intelligent, athletic, and kindhearted people. As they were growing up, we tried to balance academics with athletics. Both of our children were successful in tennis early on, but we didn't want them to sell themselves short by just focusing on that one skill.

Originally, I thought that by buying equipment and sitting in the stands, I could check off that "involved dad" box on my list of accomplishments and move on. It turns out that family needs a lot more attention on a consistent basis to feel supported.

As a parent watching my children, I wanted them to win every time. I was angry when they could not execute. The kids were young, and my wife didn't understand what I was going through. Everything that you learn from your parents gets handed down almost unconsciously.

I am a first-generation immigrant, and my parents, from my perspective, were different than American parents. We had corporal punishment, and that's how I learned. I only had my parents to look up to when it came to dealing with my own kids. But everything I learned from my parents was ineffective or inconsequential. Being physical, being angry, or being emotional just doesn't work. I read the Bible, and as a believer, I just failed to act in a manner that was "slow to anger."

The worst experience was when my daughter came right out and said, "I hate you." You will never know how low you've sunk until you hear those words coming from your child's mouth. In the past, I might have gotten angry. I could have turned my back, slammed a door in her face, or worse. But my leadership mentality kicked in; finally, and I was able to respond proactively.

"Why do you say that?" I offered. "Tell me how you feel. I'm listening."

Communication is a two-way street, whether it's in your living room or in the conference room. Respect has to be earned. As a father, I needed to respect my daughter enough to give her the floor.

I lost several million dollars on the car dealership, not to mention all the time I invested that could have been better spent with my family. That was my greatest failure, prioritizing work above the people in my life and adopting leadership traits that matter.

My key takeaways from this chapter are to listen to how you sound from the outside. It took me hearing my own words from another parent's mouth to understand how I was being perceived by my children. I was blind to it before.

And it's never too late to invest the time and energy in your family. Whether you missed practices or proms, your kids need you. Being a parent is a special kind of leadership, one that is much more enduring than any CEO position.

Don't get so caught up in making a living that you forget to live your life.

CHAPTER 10

BEING INVITED TO TRY AGAIN

Remember that light bulb moment from the last chapter? Well, forget it. I'm not a man who is built to stay at home. I was determined to do a better job at supporting my kids and my wife, but I wasn't going to do it from the living room.

After I sold my last company and made a failed personal investment, I got calls from a bunch of private equity firms. They were asking me to help turn around some of the companies in their portfolios.

But before we get to that, let's talk about something called Profit Interest Units (PIUs) in the oil and gas industry.

Let's say you own a piece of land, and you bought it for $1,000, because you want to drill for oil. From the moment you begin this venture, the land starts depreciating. Ordinarily, when an asset loses value, it's a cause for concern, but not in the context of land designed for drilling.

The more oil you manage to extract, the less the land is worth due to drilling and other activities. You might think this is a setback, but it's quite the opposite. It's like a seesaw — as one side goes down, the other goes up.

This balance between the diminishing land value and the oil extracted is crucial. It's what is referred to as PIUs. When you initially invest in this venture, you've factored in this depreciation. So, as the land's value decreases, your profits from the oil extraction increase.

Think of it as a unique synergy between the land's devaluation and the black gold you're extracting from beneath it. Understanding the industry is critical to leveraging gains. You've got to find that sweet spot where the land's value and the oil extracted intersect to yield the highest profits.

How does this relate to my story?

The concept of PIUs, despite being rooted in the oil and gas industry, is exactly the type of thing I was dealing with after the car dealership went belly up. I was being actively recruited by executive headhunters, and I was offered my choice of five different ventures. So even though I failed to manage the immoral team at the car dealership, the fact that I tried put me in a good position going forward. Even though my stake in the dealership depreciated, I was offered a wealth of new career opportunities.

During this phase of my life, I was extremely jaded. After my experience with the less than honest salespeople and the corruption that ran rampant at my auto dealership, the lack of transparency at NexusTek, the inability of private equity to act timely, and my own personal, familial fails, I had all but thrown in the towel on humanity.

If a company looked good, it was just because they were better at hiding the ugliness better than most. If they looked really good, then they were flat out liars. Profit interests in oil and gas where one side increases while the other side decreases seemed to sum up my mentality. In fact, that was the jaded belief going into the next phase of my professional career.

WASTED OPPORTUNITIES

Many of the companies I was pitched had 30-40% EBITDA margins. My skepticism kicked in — I felt those margins must be "juiced" and didn't trust the stated financials.

The private equity guys were confused. They expected me to be like all of the other mid-career leaders, interested in smooth sailing. But having just lost a few million dollars, I was in a "trust no one" mindset. I just didn't believe those numbers could be real.

In my warped mindset, I assumed that at a certain level, most people in whatever industry cared about profits over people. Whether it was telecommunications, auto sales, or oil and gas, everyone was out to make a buck. And after playing that game for so long, I was done. I was fed up with greed and all of its consequences.

I wanted to turn around a business, not just grow for growth's sake. I started looking for diamonds in the rough — good businesses with potential beyond the numbers.

LOCKER RENTALS

One of the high-growth, high-margin companies I was offered had a unique niche. I didn't end up going with them, but their concept intrigued me. The company provided locker rentals, stroller rentals, umbrella rentals, and other services inside theme parks and carnivals.

They had revenue share agreements with Walt Disney and other major theme parks and a captive customer base once people were inside. It was a very profitable business with around 42% EBITDA margins. On the books, it was growing revenues around 40% year-over-year.

I'd been to a few theme parks myself with my children. Lockers were almost imperative for families that didn't want to carry around all their belongings. Especially in water-based theme parks where mothers and fathers might have watches and wallets they didn't want to get wet. So, there was a huge customer need for the service.

At the same time, the numbers struck me as being almost too good. While I accepted the premise that most visitors to a theme park would choose to rent one or more of the company's assets, there was that little voice inside my head that warned me to stay away.

If the company was really on that kind of growth trajectory, why did they need me? I wasn't looking for a position where I could sit back, kick my feet up, and rake in the dough. I wanted to make a difference, to build on an honest premise.

Even allowing for the possibility that the company was as promising as it seemed, that wasn't something I wanted to do. Despite the seemingly incredible opportunity, it didn't align with my interests and turnaround abilities. It represented the type of high-flying business I was wary of after being burned. I passed on it. And as I did so, I realized that in some way I had become self-actualized. I had a better understanding of what I wanted.

Growing up, it was important to fit in. I wanted to be better than everyone else and succeed in sports and later, at West Point.

I thought that I was the smartest guy in the room for a while, until I realized that I wasn't. And now, I finally understood that turnaround work gave me satisfaction. My leadership style was all about helping companies and the employees who work hard in those companies get better. I also wanted to mentor employees to work successfully, not just pad the bank accounts. The kind of hyper-growth indicated by the rental company's financials wouldn't give me fulfilment, so I went in another direction.

ONEPATH HOLDINGS

I gravitated toward distressed, underperforming companies instead of highflyers. I wanted to dig into the details and turn things around, not just grow at any cost. Hypergrowth, to me, is a legend, a myth.

I'd suffered too many war wounds to go chasing the almighty dollar again. It wasn't just about how much money I could make, and it was no longer about creating my own workplace culture. Both of my previous ventures soured me and gave me a dose of reality.

This time, I wanted to start with something that I could make an impact. Like the investors in the oil and gas industry, I wanted to take a business with hidden potential and find a way to make it profitable.

I was selective and turned down several other opportunities that didn't feel like the right fit before choosing one. The company I chose was called OnePath Holdings, which had five business units and was struggling after being acquired. Each unit operated separately. Two divisions were closing down, one was losing money month-over-month, and one had nothing to do with the others. It was a mess!

However, as soon as I had a chance to connect with a few of the existing leaders in the business, I knew I'd found my diamond in the rough. It wasn't the sexiest opportunity, but it fit my skills. The people in the business worked hard. The executive suite was let go in its entirety and needed some stability. Select employees and some of the subsequent frontline managers had raw talent *and* a moral compass. One of the employees that I met was working 14-hour days to fulfill customer needs. They focused on their customers instead of lining their own pockets. They wanted to be a part of something greater than themselves.

The company had been bought for approximately $200 million but was now worth at best $75 million — a big loss for the private equity firm. EBITDA margins had declined from 12% to below 6% since the acquisition. It was clearly not inflating its worth, and I saw the dismal ROI as evidence of honesty. The people I found working there in addition to the investors were committed to telling the truth no matter what the cost.

In addition, the substandard level of operations would act like the see-saw of depreciating land value which, if nurtured properly, could generate the PIUs if the company could just find a way to pivot.

I developed a plan to shut down the low performing business units, transfer the employees who wanted to stay to the performing business units, pay down the existing debt, raise new capital, augment the executive team with new leaders, and right the ship. It seemed like a lot of work, but the culture of those that I interviewed kept me very interested. Before my final offer, I put the finishing touches on a proposal and presented the plan to the board of directors.

I was adamant that I was only going to accept the CEO role if the board went along with my suggestions. I didn't want to sit back and collect a paycheck. If they were going to bring me on board, I had to have full autonomy. The investment group agreed.

MORE HWANGISMS

My previous business failures and investments, along with my family experiences, shaped my leadership approach and helped me self-actualize into a turnaround leader. And with every successive failure, I got closer to understanding what my purpose was. I developed a few lessons learned through my Hwangisms.

1. KNOW YOURSELF

To know what you like, you have to know who you are first. This is one of my favorite lessons to share with employees and family alike. It sounds simple, but it's really not. Figuring out who you are is a lifelong process.

I've examined my life from early childhood to the peak of my career, and you should too. Some things you learn early, like the fact that being made fun of sucks. Some things take decades to learn like a healthy respect for due diligence.

I realized that I am skilled at turnarounds, and that I'm not satisfied with the status quo. I learned that being second in command of a superyacht isn't as exciting as launching my own fishing boat. I learned that my passion is to mentor and coach.

I also learned that at the end of the day, I need to be able to trust the people I work with. Nothing else is going to motivate me.

I love the back and forth with my team over how to improve operations. I have a lot of experience, and I enjoy being in a position where I can leverage that experience to provide additional impact to others.

I selected OnePath because I understood my strengths and interests, and it wasn't just about chasing money. Self-knowledge guides good decisions. I was done with the Wolf of Wall Street part of my life. It wasn't personally or professionally satisfying anymore.

I realized that I gravitated towards cynicism and wanted proof points. I needed a clear view of potential issues in "too good to be true" deals. And that skepticism kept me from risky moves.

In essence, self-actualization is an introspective process to deeply understand your talents, style, motivations, and values. This self-knowledge gained through failure allows you to make wise choices aligned with your identity and strengths.

I also developed clarity on who I was as a leader after multiple failures. Self-awareness brings confidence, which was ironically something I had been lacking before. In all my previous ventures, I assumed that I was right and that I knew what I was getting myself into. But after getting knocked down repeatedly, I finally came to the realization that **I didn't know everything** and that's absolutely okay!

I couldn't trust "too good to be true" financials or inflated valuations. By leaning into fixer-uppers, I could start somewhere rational and work my way up from there. I could recoup the equivalent of PIUs in my next venture by going after a distressed investment and turning the negative to a positive.

But even with the potentially accurate EBITDA and profit loss analysis, I had to make sure I was getting the whole picture. I didn't simply accept OnePath's financial information. I performed my own "audit" by asking pertinent questions. Because as I learned through constant repetition, **you can't trust anyone's interpretation of the truth; rather, you had to peek under the hood and create your own narrative.** This I learned from the failure of the dealership.

2. KICK THE TIRES

When attempting any kind of major transactions, you have to kick the tires. You won't know if they are good tires unless you put them to the simple test of kicking the rubber. Do your due diligence. Ask about the operating needs, cash, financial statements, and banking scenarios.

Leaders — if someone *doesn't* ask for this, be suspicious. Anyone looking to buy or invest who doesn't want to know the full picture may not be above board. Due diligence works both ways. In this instance, I was the one coming in to lead the charge. But I expected OnePath to look at me the same way.

They had an equal right to know what I was planning to do with the company. That's why I brought my game plan to the initial interview. And while I was being transparent with my intentions, I needed to know the specifics behind their losses.

3. KNOW THE RFC (REAL F'ING CASH)

Understand the true cash required to run the day-to-day transactions of business. Don't rely on projections alone. Ask for current cash balances and projected cash flow statements. Cash is king, so know the real liquidity situation.

Review full income statements, balance sheets, etc. not just highlights. Look for inconsistencies that are red flags.

4. LEARN ABOUT CURRENT BANKING RELATIONSHIPS AND COVENANTS

I uncovered that the company had already breached covenants twice. This wasn't information they were forthcoming with, and if I hadn't asked, I might not have learned the truth before taking the helm.

Uncovering that bit of information made me *more* confident in my choice, not less so. I knew there would be a lot of work to do. It was preferable to a perfect, rapidly scaling company where all the skeletons were still in the closet.

I insisted that the private equity firm be committed to more capital to fix OnePath, and they agreed.

By demanding transparency around the true financial position and ownership commitment, I was able to move forward confidently. Any strong leader should automatically ask these questions. If not, you likely don't understand the full picture.

Probing for details shows financial acumen. And if your potential partners are unwilling to share, that's an automatic red flag.

I filtered opportunities based on self-knowledge, passion, and capabilities, not just money or prestige. Values matter. I knew how to fix OnePath because I knew myself and after asking the tough questions, I had a better insight into the company.

By now, you're familiar enough with my story to know that it was not smooth sailing going forward. Once I decided on OnePath, there were more challenges in store. It wasn't my leadership that needed fixing this time, but that of my direct report. And I was about to find out just how challenging it could be to mentor someone who wasn't ready for a real leadership position.

CHAPTER 11

GAPS IN LEADERSHIP

Like a parent that has to have the crucial conversations about drugs, sex, and even friends, leaders also must be able to have crucial conversations with their employees. Unlike family, employees sometimes face severe consequences that may include termination of employment. As I took the leadership helm at OnePath, I recognized an empathetic and well-loved leader that just could not hold their employees accountable. I was less than three weeks on board a new company, and I was just getting the lay of the land. I called my VP in to talk about the salesforce. I noticed that one guy hadn't made quota for five quarters.

We had to let him go.

My sales vice president and I had a conversation that went something like this:

I said, "How is our sales team doing? Is there a reason that underperformance becomes the acceptable norm? How do we address this and hold underperforming salespeople accountable? Is there a gap or additional resources that we need to provide to ensure our sales team's success?"

The sales leader responded with, "They are all just coming up to the next level and I am confident that everyone will make quota in the next few quarters."

I asked, "The standards seem very loose, have you reiterated what is acceptable and not acceptable?"

The VP shrugged and looked a little sheepish. "I've spoken to all of the salespeople on more than one occasion, but I haven't written it up or formalized a standard."

Because it's important to follow the employee handbook, we instituted the entire termination process, and it took us three weeks. We sent underperforming salespeople a verbal and a written warning. If they were unable to remediate the underperformance, they then received a final warning. I also instructed my leadership team that if remediation was not possible, then we should be ready to terminate any salesperson. It was not personal; it was objective.

The sales leader confirmed that he was willing and able to carry the message and execute. He also apologized to me that it should have been done already, but with all of the turmoil of senior level turnover, he was not focused on those elements. Instead, he chose to focus on keeping the integrity of a positive culture. I absolutely empathized and appreciated his response.

In a few days, the sales leader called me to "chat." He mentioned that there was one employee on the sales team that pushed back on the expectations of achieving quota and had not shown up for work in a week. I asked our sales leader, "Have you fully documented and contacted our Human Resources department for next steps? I would assume that your employee should be terminated at this point."

My sales leader confided in me. "I've never fired anyone."

I went into my mentorship mode and gave him a few things he could say to make the process go smoother. "Just keep it short. Say something like, 'Hey, Brian, your performance is unacceptable and has been unacceptable. We talked about this. I wish you the best, but your services are no longer needed in our business.'"

After conferring with our vice president of human resources, she agreed that the next logical step was to terminate the sales representative's employment. As a best practice, it was necessary to have a witness and as part of the mentoring process, I agreed to be the witness during the sales representative's termination meeting.

I suggested that the VP be direct, not insulting but clear about where we stood. He said he understood what needed to be done. We went through the itinerary of his part and my observation. He confirmed and acknowledged his comprehension of the procedural aspects of the meeting. But I could tell that our sales leader was getting nervous.

The minute we got Brian, the underperforming sales representative, alone in a room, all of that preparation went out the window.

"Isn't there an HR person who can do this?" my sales leader whispered to me.

I shook my head. And instead of buckling down and doing what had to be done, the sales leader turned back to Brian. "James has something he wants to talk to you about," he said.

Then the sales leader left the room.

"Sorry about that," I said. "Give me a second." I checked to see if the sales leader was still in the hallway, but he was gone. It looked like I was on my own, and that I had been promoted from witness to deliverer of bad news. "This is probably very personal for our sales leader," I addressed our problem employee once I realized the sales leader wasn't coming back. "But we're going let you go this morning. Your results are just not there. I wish you the best of luck. This is something that I won't tolerate, and we need better production. HR will lead you through the exit process. Any questions?"

"I understand," Brian said, and he left without any drama. Afterward, I hunted down the sales leader to make it known that I was not pleased with his inability to step up to the plate.

By walking out of the room, the sales leader didn't save Brian's job. He just told me through his actions that he wasn't up to the task of leadership...not yet. If you can't have hard conversations with people, how are you going to show them the way in times of crisis?

WHEN YOU DON'T HAVE A SPOONFUL OF SUGAR
That incident was a very clear failure of leadership. My sales leader and I had a very long talk afterwards.

"Look," he said, "I've never really had to go through that process before. I typically talk to my guys, and they exit gracefully over some period of time," the sales leader exclaimed.

I appreciate the sentiment and how hard it is to let someone go, but the fact remains that being in charge comes with some tough situations. Put yourself in the business owner's shoes. You're expecting the person you hired to lead to make sure things are progressing smoothly. No business owner wants to be giving handouts to underproductive employees. It's a business and if someone isn't making their quota quarter after quarter, then you need to coach them or let that person go.

Yes, it's hard. It *should* be hard. I don't mean to be a jerk about it. If you really analyze the situation, you're doing both people a disservice by keeping someone on who isn't happy and not performing. In that type of situation where it's clear that they're hanging on by a thread, it's not in anyone's best interest to keep the status quo.

You might be restricting your problem employee from achieving their own goals. Underperformance is a sure sign of dissatisfaction. If they're on the wrong bus, they need to find a bus that's going to a location suitable for them.

Delivering good news is easy. Everyone's happy, you can stand up in front of the group and say, "Congratulations, you did an awesome job. Here's your gold medal!"

Letting someone go is a much harder discussion. In my opinion, leaders that don't know how to terminate haven't failed enough. Ultimately, the sales leader had to let go of two more people that were in that same situation. One did not produce at all for eight months. The second one didn't even make one sale in the last six months, nor did he have any outstanding proposals.

The sales leader, however, was the favorite of the entire sales team and some service employees. He was the proverbial teddy bear, loved and hugged by all. The sales vice president was incredibly uncomfortable in the role of enforcer as he just wanted to care for everyone. I sat in with him on both of the termination meetings and they went on much longer than they should have. It should be a five-minute meeting or less. Just like I laid it out for Brian letting him know that this isn't working, we needed to part ways.

It's hard for people to understand that, because a lot of people have never given someone their walking papers. When you fumble that, it can be tough to recover. Whether it's a performance improvement plan, or that first termination, dealing effectively with crucial conversations separates leaders from managers. Additionally, for the performers in the group, the negative consequences for non-performing personnel actually improve the morale of the entire team. Respect and integrity of the team comes through positive awards as well as negative consequences. As long as the application of the outcomes are equitable, fair, and transparent, the entirety of the team improves when crucial conversations occur, awards are publicly administered, and negative consequences are privately and swiftly executed.

STACK RANK
Introduced by General Electric's CEO Jack Welch in the 1980s, stack ranking is a talent management strategy where employees are evaluated and classified on a bell curve as exemplary, meeting

expectations, or needing improvement. In this system, a fixed number of employees can be considered high-performing. This approach motivated employees to outperform their peers, as those in the bottom 15% faced potential layoffs.[20]

That's the dictionary definition.

Here's my take. If you have a team, you probably already know how your players stack up. Yes, go to the data, but if you've spent any time listening to sales calls or walking the floor, you're probably 90% sure how the ranking will go down.

Jack Welch said that you need to support your top group by letting go of the bottom. Keeping the underperformers on the team for a prolonged time creates negative reinforcement for the overachievers. If you want that top group and the median group to reach for the stars, that bottom group must improve or be let go. The chemistry and the adoration for performance can only be created when every member of the team has the same vision and a similar work ethic. The strong performers tend to get stronger when they are pushed to strive for even more, especially if they are in a climate that awards top performance.

Every good leader needs to be able to observe and orient their staff to prevent settling among the top tier. Try this the next time you're in a meeting with middle managers. Ask them who their top performers are. They'll brag about them all day long. Then ask them who their bottom performers are and watch them clam up. If they're reluctant to give you that information, then there's a problem.

---

[20] Tansey, C. January 5, 2023. What Is 'Stack Ranking' and Why Is It a Problem? (lattice.com)

People like my sales vice president want to hide behind the concept of altruism. They want to pretend that everything is going well, and that everyone is pulling their own weight. "My team is awesome," he'll claim.

I get that. *But I want your team to become even better.* Identifying the weakest link is important to the structural integrity of the entire chain. And maybe you're going to have to fire that person, but it doesn't do the organization any good to protect them.

Likewise, in the military, they force rate you on a scale of one to five. If you don't get in the top two segments, you don't get promoted. If you rank in the bottom two, you're not going to get renewed. Jack Welch may have taken that concept and transformed it into something that could be used in the commercial sector. The long game is that if you've got good players, you have to support them. If you've got bottom feeders, then you need to rotate them out. And it may not feel good, but it benefits the company in the end.

There's an old saying that there's a three to one tributary effect when you're making staffing decisions. When you lay off ten people, there are thirty people at risk. People talk, and workspaces are by definition social environments. For each person you lay off, there are three good friends, mentors, or padawans who might decide to leave with them.

This works great if the other two people are also in the bottom third, but not so well if your firing decision robs you of a high achiever. So, this is something you need to keep in mind when making staff changes. I'm not saying that you should hang onto those ten problem employees. Far from it. I'm just pointing out what your HR department already knows so that you can be aware going in.

You have to be able to terminate people individually. No matter how much you tout your "family" atmosphere, or believe in the inherent goodness of people, sometimes it just doesn't work out. Then you have to make the decision as to whether the bottom performers are enough of a liability to let them go.

Firing is never easy. It isn't fun to ruin someone's day, but in the end, your company will be better for it. And while some people might be blindsided by the action you take, most will realize that something has gone wrong long before you invite them into your office.

By terminating their employment, you open up a window for them to move on to the next phase of their lives. They're probably not happy where they are, and they need to try something else. By approaching it that way, you can give yourself permission to have that difficult conversation. Don't run out of the kitchen when it gets hot. That's no way to demonstrate actionable leadership.

So, what makes for a good leader? We've talked a lot about learning from failure and how to leverage your challenges to build your competency. But now let's take a moment to really dive into one example of poor leadership skills. In this case, the person wasn't a soft old teddy bear who wanted to see everyone succeed. He was actively lying to me, but by the time I realized it, a great deal of damage had already been done.

CHAPTER 12

MAKING THE DIFFICULT BUT RIGHT DECISION

I once hired a person who came with a spectacular referral, and I eventually had to terminate him. He wasn't just a salesperson. He was the chief operating officer for our managed services division and he came highly recommended by a personal friend.

By the time he came to me, three out of my nine key leaders had already touched base, and they loved him. I liked him too in the beginning. But if I'm being honest, there was something that never sat right.

THE FIRST PROBLEM: LEADERSHIP STYLE
My failure in this example was that I didn't go with my gut. My decision was based on emotion and momentum. I should have explored more about why I felt that way and what it was about this star candidate that rubbed me wrong. I've taken a similar approach to John Maxwell,[21] which I'll go into further in the final chapter. I distill his five-stage leadership framework into four

---

21 Maxwell, J. C. (2021). *5 levels of leadership: Proven steps to maximize your potential.* CENTER ST.

key stages: positional, relational, pragmatic, and mentorship. John Maxwell's influence has a clear impact in my framework, but I added the calluses from various failures throughout my career. I call my framework *Actionable Leadership*.

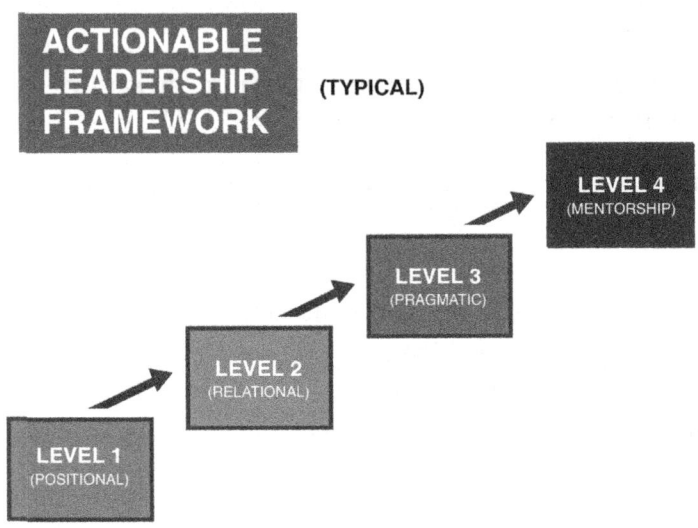

Positional leadership is the influence a leader exerts due to their rank. It is the lowest level of leadership but it's necessary. It's a position thing and nothing else. Because of the interview, past experiences, tenure, or other merit worthy elements, the leadership level of "position" is conveyed to the person. As far as influence goes, it is minimal at best. The only exemption to this adage is in the military.

Rank in the military, regardless of influence, respect, or even acrimonious feelings towards the higher ranked position, comes with a sense of accountability. In the private sector, leadership and rank can be parallel constructs. However, leadership and rank from a positional standpoint is not parallel at its starting point. Once a person has position, they have the obligation and opportunity to increase influence through leadership. Otherwise, it's a reversion to a lackluster, dictatorial, military-like state where the followers are only going through the motions.

The relational leadership level is the next stage where the emphasis is in getting to know your employees. If you don't know your employees, if you don't know their middle names, their wives' first name, their children, then they're not going to be invested in you. They are not going to trust you. They may perform satisfactorily, but you're not going to get the invitation to trust unless a relationship is formed.

People are influenced primarily through trust, making it a necessary component of any workplace to achieve 100% buy in. That's why I share some of my own personal details with people I have led. I find that by establishing common ground through family stories or even stories of failure, I can open my office door, so to speak, and create an atmosphere of trust and build a lasting relationship.

Pragmatic leadership is the ability to influence others through trust and take the necessary actions to achieve a task, objective, or mission. Pragmatic levels are achieved when a leader can ask a team member to try new things and the follower is confident to exercise new approaches knowing that the environment is safe and that no negative repercussions will come their way. It is a symbiotic relationship where trust from the leader allows team members to go act and the team members confidently perform in such a way that their leader will not find fault but create a safe workplace to try new things. Mentorship is the fourth level of the Actionable Leadership framework, and it is what all leaders should be working toward. We're going to cover each of these stages in much more detail in the next chapter, but I will say that mentors are incredibly valuable. These are folks who have achieved so much that they can turn around and share those experiences with others. They aren't worried about being the smartest person in the room or about forcing people to do things their way. They guide their subordinates toward making the right decisions through accumulated wisdom.

The new managed services COO's style of leadership was very much binary. He operated almost like a computer, with ones and zeros, but nothing else. He saw the world in black and white, but good leaders have to be comfortable operating in the grey. He performed very well for twelve months. The last three months, unfortunately, he was picking fights with East/West partners. It was partly my fault because I was forcing that East/West concept.

But he had his own yardstick that was either right or wrong. He would approach the sales team with an attitude that said, "You're not doing it the way I told you to, therefore, you're a zero. I'm a one. I am right." There were only two options.

Not only were the team members within his organization leaving the company, but he was having the same impact on the East/West corridor. It was his way or the highway. He lacked the relational aspect of leadership and kept gravitating towards the positional level of influence. In other words, he was dictating without creating a relationship.

My failure was in not hiring someone who had a complimentary approach to leadership. There may not be a "right" way to lead, but you definitely have to build a team that works together. If you have a relational style, one can typically mend misunderstandings or be invited to discuss further. Positional players tend to have expectations for what their subordinates *should* do. The leader assumes that they know exactly what should be done and how. The relational leader has the sense of humility and understands that leaders can learn from subordinates and subordinates are invited to respectfully and constructively push so that the entire team becomes better... including the leader.

THE SECOND PROBLEM: STAFF TURNOVER

I'll call the new COO Isaac. He was well known in the technology space and very well admired by others. In fact, he was an advisor to many other smaller companies. It was an honor for me to recruit a person like that into our group. I shared the interview process with all the department leaders, and everyone initially loved the guy. But my failure was in not vetting him completely. He sailed through the interview with just a few questions. I made the hiring decision based on the recommendations I got and my overall sense of him as a friend. I put him in charge of the service delivery platforms, and everything else in the company with the exception of sales and finance.

Initially, it was great to see him integrate. His core values and his personality seemed to connect with the existing engineering team and his direct reports. But then something suspicious began to happen. We turned over somewhere north of 20% of our outstanding technicians in a 1,000-person company. That's two hundred people.

When I confronted him, he said, "That's because we don't offer competitive wages and quite frankly the engineers that were here were average at best."

It was true, we didn't pay the best wages; but we didn't pay the worst. We also promoted many new engineer apprentices from an entry level call center position. His suggestion had some truth to it, but we didn't investigate further. Many new leaders create some exodus of existing players for cultural fit or different career aspirations. Also, the tech industry typically fielded an annual turnover rate in the mid 20% so we weren't that much higher than the average.

My first failure was that I didn't follow through and investigate further. I should have done a better job in gauging the morale of the employees. And for me, the additional failure in that episode became another Hwangism..."Inspect what you expect." I didn't inspect.

Despite what you might think from my military experience and my challenging childhood, I trust everyone. That's a fine way to live, but you've got to do your homework. I let all the good things I'd heard about Isaac cloud my judgement. It didn't occur to me that he was the reason we were losing so many employees.

About a year before COVID, I had to focus on four other divisions of the company as part of our strategic business plan. I was going to divest the other divisions and focus on the key, core asset of IT managed services. The division of which Isaac was the chief operating officer was hemorrhaging information technology-centric engineers. I left Isaac in full trust of his group to manage while I executed on the strategic divestitures. Little did I know, this would lead to my next failure.

THE THIRD PROBLEM: NUMBERS

Even though I was out of the office working with investment bankers, I diligently checked in with key leaders to understand day-to-day performance. I also had the opportunity to review our key performance metrics and financials. I noticed we were stagnating in our high growth division of managed services. We had all these efficiency initiatives and multiple sales bookings, but the numbers didn't play out. We were treading water with our earnings growing slightly but not at the levels that I would have expected.

With the focus on divestitures, I think the board was okay with that small growth in the managed services division. But in the back of my mind, I knew that something was not right. At the highest bookings level, Isaac was talking about all these wins. But if costs decreased and revenues increased like he suggested, gross margins should have increased, and our EBITDA should have been exploding.

That was my initial gut feeling and my logic was substantiating this hypothesis.

I was heavily engaged in the processes of divesting other portions of the business. We consolidated two divisions into one and sold that to a telecom company. We also sold another division of approximately 200 employees to a low voltage expert. These outcomes proved to be better than expected as the market during COVID and right afterwards saw valuations through the roof. We paid off the majority of our debt and gained additional commitments of capital for our managed services division. We fully anticipated executing multiple acquisitions with this capital facility expansion. In the process, we also closed an international division that was losing money. In all, our strategic execution was better than expected and it presented a tremendous opportunity for our remaining, core division of managed services primed for success. So, I thought.

In one of our first staff meetings, post final divestiture, I asked Isaac, "Hey, what's going on? We should be making money hand over fist."

"Oh, James, you don't understand," he said. "You've been kind of distant. We had a lot of turnover."

That would explain the depressed figures, but it didn't get to the heart of the matter.

"So, what's creating that turnover?" I asked.

He didn't have an answer for that. He tried to push it off on the industry, or on the wages we were paying our staff. I saw things a little differently. I realized that I left Isaac in control of the store while I went out to sell the other businesses. I trusted him, but he hadn't earned that trust. He was too new to the organization, and he hadn't been vetted.

He didn't even go through a proper interview process. It was just me and several close allies having a conversation. We skipped the necessary procedures and that left us vulnerable to a person whose style became toxic.

Around that time, I noticed some shady practices in Isaac's financial management. Revenue was increasing, but I suspected something wasn't right about the way Isaac handled the company's finances and customer interactions.

We looked at reports frequently, analyzing monthly business reviews and checking the bottom line. Despite positive numbers in bookings and cash flow, there were discrepancies between bookings and billings, indicating churning of clients or failed implementations.

Working with the divisional finance leaders, I introduced a method to audit the activation and invoicing process.

	Assigned to a staff member?	Activated?	Invoiced?	
	1	1	0	Assigned, activated, but not invoiced
Red Flag	1	0	1	Assigned, not activated but invoiced
	1	1	1	Assigned, activated, and invoiced

The three-tier audit as it became known, is another Hwangism. The three-tier audit is simply (1) What is booked versus authorized, (2) What is authorized versus billed, and (3) What is billed versus procured. The three-step process for me is to align sales, to service, to procurement. What was sold? What is activated? What is invoiced? And just as important, for each billable element, what is the matching cost. When we can perform this triple-tier audit, most of the revenue and cost assurance concerns are mitigated.

With an audit function such as this, it became evident that some clients were being billed for services they didn't receive, artificially inflating profits. The issue was spotted when a new controller compared the number of licenses to actual users, revealing a significant discrepancy.

We discovered about $900,000 of annual licensing expenses that were never deactivated, leading to financial losses and compromised services. This was the actual reason that gross margins hadn't increased. This was a major area of discrepancy in the EBITDA, not just the company turnover.

That was my first concrete finding with Isaac.

I couldn't believe he had orchestrated the whole thing. And I said, "Isaac, this is a big issue, right? We have to fix this."

I had all the faith in the world in him, but we had to fix it. Now that we had a new controller, we had the wherewithal to right the ship. But in the back of my mind, I had to consider the fact that Isaac knew all along.

He said, "We'll get around to it."

I said, "We should get to it. It should be a top priority issue! Do you not agree?" He acknowledged its importance with a simple nod.

The difference was nearly a million dollars, and we just identified it. Afterwards, the numbers started to pick up a bit, but we were still left with the turnover problem. I asked Isaac if he conducted any exit interviews. He said to me that he did not and that was a function of HR. There was the positional leadership level blaring a huge siren at me. If Isaac believed that HR should be the only people conducting exit interviews, then he was creating a "this is not my job" approach. As leaders, we need to strive to increase our influence by taking it beyond the positional level to the next wrung of relational. I kept asking myself, "Why wasn't he meeting with people? Why wasn't he trying to identify the source of the problem?"

Isaac said he spoke with seven people that were employed at that time. He had over a hundred and twenty-five on his staff. Also, he turned over more than fifty people from his business unit alone.

He assured me that he would get around to it. Eventually, we heard from some of the people who left. And I took that feedback to heart.

One of the former employees said, "Hey, James, you know I still love the company. It just wasn't for me. Not at that time. I trust you, but I don't know if I can trust the other leaders of the organization."

THE FOURTH PROBLEM: SECURITY BREACH

Another terrifying thing that happened that I could lay at Isaac's doorstep is that some of the folks who were leaving still had access to our company accounts. We found out because someone told us. The ex-employee in question wasn't upset with me, but he left because of Isaac's managerial style. He found out he could still log on and contacted me personally to give me the heads up.

This was a critical mistake because depending on the scruples of the person who had walked away, they could have done some real damage. I felt like I hired legendary NBA coach Phil Jackson but he wasn't performing at all.

The guy who clued us into the security breach didn't really want to leave. I gather he felt so disconnected with the management and the leadership, that he couldn't hang on. He had a better offer, and he took it.

The security lapse occurred because Isaac failed to submit the termination paperwork timely. When Isaac turned in the paperwork, some of them were delayed by two to three weeks! That meant the employee who was resigning had access to our systems and was receiving a paycheck well beyond their last days of employment. With the security lapse, I asked my chief technology officer (CTO), a trusted veteran of the industry, to lead a small team to conduct a security audit and remediation effort. Randy is not only a veteran but a superb leader who has proven himself to wield not just the positional and relational levels of influence, but also the next level of influence: pragmatic.

Randy was the epitome of pragmatism at work. He was able to create a five-person task team and within three weeks, audit the network, reconcile the users, patch our network environment, create a new security protocol, and train the entirety of the engineering and administrative staff on the new process. The five-person team and Randy, together, worked with new tools and designed new processes from scratch. I personally had the chance to observe them and thank them for their critical efforts. Randy would work side-by-side with each of the members, coaching, directing, observing, and auditing. This was pragmatism in action!

STAGING AN INTERVENTION
In the middle of this crisis, we started to see infighting between Isaac and the rest of the leadership team. As I was

putting pressure on Isaac, the people who recommended him, who sat in on the hiring meeting with me, started to say, "What is going on here?"

We had all trusted him. And not one of us did the due diligence to check out his previous companies. Isaac at that point told me that he had some mental health concerns he needed to prioritize. He took some time off. It dragged out far longer than it should have.

When Isaac returned in two weeks, I decided to have an intervention. We were committed to Isaac. There were several executives who wanted to participate, and we all got together and said, "We love you, man. But things have got to change."

The intervention didn't go well.

You would think that a person returning from two weeks off would be refreshed. Isaac was not. He turned on us and got abusive. "You guys suck!" he shouted. "You guys have it all wrong!" Isaac pointed a finger at me but continued to berate the other four executives in the room. The tirade went on for several minutes and it was all one-sided. There was no personal culpability, accountability, or responsibility. There was only a one direction blame game. Blame everyone else.

It probably took six months from the time that I started to pick up on the issues with the customer auditing to the intervention. I was doing backflips to convince myself that he was the right leader.

It's a shame because we all would have supported him if he handled it differently. At that point, I had to let him go. I suspect he might have been dealing with something in his personal life that affected him at work. At the end of the day, I gave him the benefit of the doubt and assumed that all the headaches he gave us were unintentional. I don't believe that he was corrupt, just incompetent.

But the minute that he left, the company rebounded, culture stabilized, and productivity increased. Also, earnings went up! It was a hard lesson for me because that rebound was the exclamation point at the end of a very long sentence. It was crystal clear that I should have let him go in the very beginning. Or better yet, I should have vetted him correctly before putting all my trust in him.

The lesson was obvious. Even in the inner, trusted circle, you have to separate the personal and the professional. Working with people that I really enjoy and trust is important. But it's also important to keep the health of the company in sight.

People know when they have bad leadership. And fortunes can turn better on a dime. Trust your balanced emotions and logic when they say that something's not right. Dig deeper; go with your instincts; ask the hard questions. If I hadn't been so committed to Isaac from the get-go, I might have saved the company hundreds of employees and a lot of heartache.

HWANGISMS CONTINUED

In this segment, there are a few Hwangisms that I would offer. I had the opportunity to learn from Jim Collins directly on the importance of people first. Jim would whisper to me during our conversations that it is always "the who before the what!" This is the tenet that guides business leaders and executives to hire a leader who can be trusted and is capable of being influential before any "thing" is developed. Tangible intellectual property is important, but leaders exponentially highlight its usefulness with trust and motivation.

The second Hwangism from this segment is to "trust but verify." "Trust but verify" is the concept where leaders conduct simple and periodic audits on how people work. We hire auditors for financial audits. We hire consulting groups to conduct systems and technology audits. We have auditors, not because we don't trust our chief financial officer or our respective chief information officer; rather, these audits give assurance to the executives that we are on the right trajectory. If not, it's a great tool to course correct. So, how often do we lean into people-management audits? Such a "trust but verify" approach is critical in every level of management. This has nothing to do with a lack of trust and it shouldn't be viewed as such.

After suffering through such a blatant example of positional leadership gone wrong, you might be surprised when I jump straight to mentorship. I can only speak from experience, and I found that being a mentor myself came with a lot of rewards. In this next chapter, we'll talk about becoming a mentor and when you know it's time to let go.

CHAPTER 13

WHEN YOU OVERSTAYED YOUR WELCOME

A typical condition in a lot of M&A (mergers and acquisitions) is a continuity clause that provides incentive for the previous owner or CEO to stay on after the transaction. The idea is that the old owner will have valuable insight and historical knowledge that can benefit the buyer. The problem is that having someone around with ties to the old way of doing things only aggravates growing pains that are a necessary part of life after a merger. Furthermore, identifying the next leader who could take over for the departing owner is not an easy task.

Identifying, developing, training, and guiding through successes and failures is all about mentorship. Mentorship is not a task; it is a journey that builds on top of the positional stage of leadership. It leverages trust that is created from the relationship stage and allows influence to take shape through pragmatic efforts. In order to achieve mentorship status, one must pass through the successes and failures of doing things together. Successes build momentum and failures that invite an opportunity to learn and create a deeper level of trust.

Regardless, all that experience will help create the next leader who can provide continuity when the torch is passed.

Transitions also require a focus on leadership; leadership through the four levels of influence via positional, relational, pragmatic, and mentorship. The highest level of mentorship creates succession at the business and team levels. It also assures a smooth transition during mergers and acquisitions. Leaders who have earned a position, gotten to know their teams by building a relationship, and building trust through pragmatic actions, should be ready to elevate the next leader. This mentorship approach creates a mutual two-way trusting relationship where skills, approach, successes, and failures are shared together in anticipation that the leader moves on to the next role and the mentee becomes the new leader.

In one of the acquisitions, I retained the owner to assist in mentoring their identified leader to run the company (now a division of our combined organization). In terms of business, the owner, Craig, was strong-willed and one of those people that just had to have it his way. I used six-month contracts for continuity purposes. But what I realized was that I was extending continuity longer than I should.

While I tried to make changes, he went around and tried to set things back to the way they were. The owner of a smaller technology services company was undermining the direction of the entirety of the combined company.

In one situation, I asked that we recruit engineers utilizing our dedicated recruiters. Craig did not like this model since his company always needed to be nimble. He would hire contractors through an employment agency so he could have them be productive within a week from "ordering" the contract. The new engineer was on a contractual basis being paid at a premium rate. They appreciated opportunities to work overtime because then they were being renumerated at 1.5 to 2.0 times the already high pay rate. Even 30 days post-acquisition, the amount of contractors ballooned from 30 to 60 people. Of those 60 people, 57 worked overtime!

Craig's rationale was that if you hire contractors, you can test them before offering a permanent role. The fallacy with this thought in a company that wielded hundreds of engineers was that the costs quickly spiraled out of control. Moreover, there was no incentive for the contractor to become a permanent employee. All of the contractors were being compensated at premium hourly rates. The majority of them were working overtime. Hence, by the time the good engineers who passed Craig's "test period" were offered the permanent role, they flatly turned it down citing a 30 to 40% pay cut if they were to come on board as a full-time employee. Yet, Craig was adamant that this should be the "way!"

What I learned is that the owners needed to be vacated quickly. Mentors and mentees need to be groomed through the positional, relational, and pragmatic rituals that are governed by one single style of leadership...our leadership. A lot of these founders, and Craig in particular, were used to having things done their way. It can be nearly impossible for someone in their position to go from having all the say, to having next to none. Moreover, by keeping the previous owner around, you are inviting more tension for the staff between one set of owners and the previous owners.

CLEANING UP AFTER THE PREVIOUS OWNER

It took me a New York minute to figure out what Craig was doing in terms of the contractors. The problem presented itself as a spike in the labor costs and constant engineering turnover. I followed the money trail and sure enough, overtime dropped to zero once the contractors went to permanent positions. They became disgruntled at the pay cut and looked for other jobs. Once they found something better, they left. Money became the culprit, and the core values were non-existent.

Most of all, the client experience suffered. Many of the engineers that accepted permanent employee status became clock watchers. At 4:01 or 5:01 p.m., when their day was completed, it was like an F1 or NASCAR pit stop. They raced to their cars and left the offices before the clock could strike 4:02 or 5:02 p.m. The only ones that remained were the employees that were hired through our recruiters or were transferees from the headquarters company.

And those people who didn't leave, their morale was in the toilet. That owner definitely overstayed his welcome. I spent so much time untangling the knot he created while he was right there saying, "I don't have a clue why this is happening."

It would have been much easier to cut the umbilical cord, institute brand new policies, and take it from there.

THE NEXT ONE UP

The reality is that we kept Craig around longer than we should have. However, there wasn't anyone trained and viable to take his place. The problem that we find in many small or midsized businesses is that there are not enough leaders. There are even fewer leadership apprentices/mentees.

As I looked around to my direct staff of executives, the clear choice for taking over the acquired company had been with me for over ten years. He was a frontline manager, a second-level manager, and even a junior executive. He earned those positions due to the outstanding effort and in many cases, the successes of the roles that he was assigned. More importantly, I built a level of trust by getting to know him personally. I knew each of his three children by name and he knew my two children as well. We were always conscious of how each other's spouses would react when working late or bringing homework. We knew what would motivate each other or upset one another.

From there, we spent years working on projects together. We would set up budgets and implement them only to come back to the table sixty days later laughing about how stupid we felt for not thinking through a particular problem. We also had numerous successes in re-engineering and re-organizing the teams, divisions, and even the organization as a whole. He would mimic many of my approaches and lingos. Ironically, I would do the same. We had so many chances to try new things: some we succeeded; some we did not. This was the blending of a pragmatic and mentoring relationship as we leaned into one another for support.

I had the perfect answer to the next leader in situations where we would acquire businesses and exit the founders immediately. The answer was my mentee, Luca. It had been there all along, but I needed to fail with Craig to fully understand it.

MORE HWANGISMS

Craig's story is about "firing fast and hiring slow." Although this could be applicable with Isaac too, Craig is why I no longer keep previous business owners, especially from smaller organizations, post-acquisition. This approach actually creates better continuity as long as the mentor-mentee relationships are prioritized. In essence, if Craig was fired quickly when I realized the conflicts of authority, we would have saved hundreds of thousands of dollars and significantly cut down on our aspirin consumption.

CHAPTER 14

LEADERSHIP FRAMEWORK

Through a sampling of my failures (trust me, there's many more), I have learned so much about business, leadership, and myself. It starts with the position that one has, but building relationships must immediately become part of the leadership journey. From relationships, opportunities to work together, and a pragmatic approach, a hopeful outcome is trust.

Of course there are elements of working together that can erode trust, but as long as both leaders and followers work together, communicate East/West and are vulnerable enough to fail together, trust will build over time. Additionally, I believe that failures are necessary to shape you into an effective leader that you envision to become. You can only create leaders and become a great mentor if you have walked the same path, learned from your failures, and continued to grow even after a long list of successes. Neither failures nor successes should stop you from growing.

Here is a much more detailed explanation of my Actionable Leadership framework, developed after years of failure (and some success). This visual illustrates how trust is formed through the relational, pragmatic, and mentorship stages.

ACTIONABLE LEADERSHIP FRAMEWORK

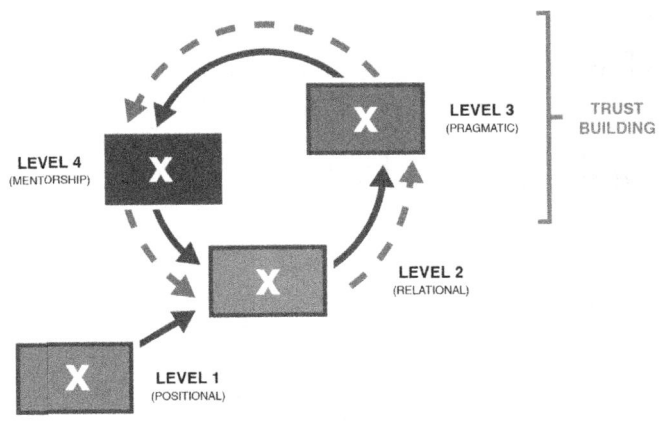

POSITIONAL LEADERSHIP – 1ST LEVEL

Positional leadership refers to the influence a leader has simply because of their **title or rank in an organization.** As CEO, I have positional power to set the vision and direction for our company. However, just having a high position does not automatically make someone a great leader. Effective positional leaders avoid just giving orders and instead empower their team to take ownership of their work.

In my own life, I had a positional leadership role at AT&T, but that didn't mean I had earned any respect from the line workers. I coined the Hwangism, "Land this boat," to mean getting a job done.

At the positional level of leadership, it is very important to complete tasks and generate outcomes. "Landing the boat" serves as a motivation for employees to get their work done on time so that the entire project can move forward. Positional leadership is a good starting point, but it should not stop there. If you can recall what happened in the story I shared in Chapter 3 when I was tasked to lead a portion of the arms sales project in Operation Desert Shield and Operation Desert Storm in the Middle East, you'd know why positional leadership does not make you a true leader. People that follow a positional leader only do so because they have to. It's the minimal level of leadership influence and it also carries minimal levels of input, care, and accountability. And just because you have the position as a leader, it doesn't mean you can expect that your people would want to follow you.

RELATIONAL LEADERSHIP – 2ND LEVEL

Relational leadership focuses on the **interpersonal connections between leaders and followers.** Strong relational leaders take time to build trust and rapport with their team members. They observe and listen first before telling team members what to do. They coach through two-way communication, asking questions, providing context, and explaining the reasoning behind requests. This type of leadership requires empathy, approachability, and consideration of employees' needs and perspectives.

I use the Hwangism of "reach around to the other side" to illustrate the importance of relational leadership. However, East/West communications as well as a new Hwangism called "escalate early and often" are tools to iterate and build relationships with peers, superiors, and subordinates.

If, as a leader, you can move your team from their individual silos to genuine collaboration, you will have done your job. Auto executive, Lee Iacocca, made a direct engagement to the employees on the ground, observed the processes, and gained insights on the operations. By immersing himself in the actual workings of the organization, he uncovered the real problems and ultimately created solutions. Just the same, after initially failing to connect with the team I was trying to help, I followed Iacocca's approach and it proved to be the best way to effectively engage people to solve the problems with you.

But while relational leadership is a step in the right direction, there is still more that you can do to motivate and inspire your team.

PRAGMATIC LEADERSHIP – 3RD LEVEL

Pragmatic leadership involves **aligning teams toward common goals through concrete actions.** Pragmatic and relational levels are looping levels and sit at the primary core of actionable leadership. Build relationships by doing things together. When two or more successes (or failures) happen, it stimulates relationships. Try it! Here are three pragmatic approaches that have worked for me:

1. **Gain consensus on end state:** Leaders and team members jointly plan milestones, define success metrics, and create scorecards to track progress. Leaders assign tasks to both themselves and team members in service of the larger objectives.
2. **Discuss required outcomes:** Leaders and team members identify and sequence necessary tasks, aligning their roles to complete the work. Leaders are open to switching roles as needed.
3. **Leader observes:** After agreeing on goals and measures, leaders step back and let team members take charge to achieve outcomes while providing feedback. As you

observe, orient, direct, and analyze, do it again and again. This too is a looping motion.

Because the focus is to produce impact, you, as a leader, must break down any barrier to communications. You use your *position* to give your team directions on what to do, and you *relate* to your team to understand what they need in order to execute. Now, you will need to make the people on the same level communicate effectively with each other. But how do you do that?

MENTORSHIP LEADERSHIP – 4TH LEVEL
Mentorship is what John Maxwell calls the "pinnacle" level. I agree. When you have the opportunity to find your next "Luca" as I did, you will pour your learnings into them. They also will teach you a thing or two. Build a safe, trustworthy environment, where problems can be discussed openly.

Effective mentors are patient, lead by example, and commit to advancing others. Mentorship leadership multiplies leadership throughout an organization. I use the Hwangism "escalate early and often" to help those I mentor. This is one of the best pieces of advice I can give anyone who is thrust into a leadership role and is seeking to build a relationship, be pragmatic, and mentor. Let them know that you are available to work together. Let them know that things will go wrong. Let them also know that at times the process is more important than the outcome.

Young leaders must first become self-aware by figuring out who they are and what they like. The best way to support your team is by giving them clear directions, and that can only be done when you know what you want to see. Mentorship involves a looping interaction between relational, pragmatic, and mentorship levels. As you tackle more tasks together, you naturally build your relationship and your mentorship.

The focus should not be on the result; rather, the spotlight should be on the approaches or processes that solve problems. Trust allows "escalating early and often" and relationships allow for East/West communications. The environment of trust sets the tone for crucial conversations and ultimately the satisfaction of great outcomes or the laughter of failures. Mentorship also involves teaching from experience without jealousy. Set up your padawan for success by helping them avoid some of the failures you've suffered, and the entire company will benefit.

VALUES-BASED LEADERSHIP
At our companies, I aim to lead with integrity, excellence, accountability, and teamwork. Although if you've read this far, you'll know that in my early years I struggled with some of these. I believe leadership stems from a sense of purpose, a "why" that drives the organization. For my company, the "why" is empowering underserved small and medium businesses by providing enterprise-level technology affordable and accessible.

Leaders should enable **action**, not just communicate vision and ideas. The concept of "servant leadership," as identified by John Maxwell where leaders focus on removing roadblocks and facilitating the work rather than just telling others what to do, is highly effective. Servant leaders exhibit modesty and avoid micromanaging once they've provided direction and support.

The final Hwangism that I'll highlight in this section is "Repeat everything seven times four different ways." This Hwangism actually applies to all levels of leadership.

By packaging every communication into different formats, you are being inclusive of everyone. Some people check their email more frequently than others. Some people will ignore every written communication but pay close attention when something comes up in a staff meeting. Still others like graphics to illustrate new policies. Whatever it is that you're trying to get across, you need to make sure you repeat it frequently.

By repeating, sometimes parceling and scheduling messages, you are doing everyone a favor by creating the foundation of comprehension that creates the groundwork for effective communications. Purposeful communications lead to comprehension. There is no such thing as overcommunicating as you guide your team members to work with each other. Repeating the messages, often through different mediums creates ample opportunities to create retention. This is by far the best way to communicate to individuals and teams.

This is by far the best way to communicate the values of your organization, and the expectations you have for your team. By overcommunicating, you guide your team members to work more efficiently with each other which is the core goal for values-based leadership.

CULTIVATING LEADERSHIP AT ALL LEVELS

A key tenet of my leadership philosophy is that leadership is not confined to people at the top but rather is the responsibility of everyone in the organization. All team members should strive to be leaders and avoid mediocrity by taking initiative, developing expertise, and collaborating effectively.

Leadership isn't just a top-down activity, either. Employees can spot a bad leader as soon as they walk in the door. They need to take responsibility for pushing back against substandard leadership. Whether that looks like going to HR or having a difficult meeting with their new manager, they shouldn't just passively follow or assume that the company will take one side or another.

Team members should demand observable competence and character from their leaders. They deserve leaders who engage in clear communication, welcome feedback, take responsibility for mistakes, and focus on collective success.

When all team members embrace leadership behaviors, they become more invested and empowered to drive the organization forward. Leadership must be actionable at every level, not just demonstrated by those at the top. By leaning into their own leadership potential, team members multiply an organization's capability exponentially.

CONCLUSION

"It's not just about getting back up but learning, tweaking, and not being afraid of failing again. Several management best practices have come from this approach."

— **James Hwang**

Angela Duckworth talks about grit as being a key ingredient in success. She defines it as the ability to sustain interest and effort over the long term.

I agree that grit is necessary, but I think there's more to it than that. I've failed again and again over the course of my life. Revisiting the past, I can confidently say that I've learned something from every failure. Here is a summary of my twelve lessons learned:

1. Taking the short bus taught me that I had no tolerance for losing.
2. One of my direct reports shitting in a helicopter taught me to pay more attention to the morale of the troops.
3. Assuming that I was the smartest person in the room taught me that I wasn't.

4. An unquenchable thirst for the almighty dollar taught me to get my priorities straight.
5. Losing my moral compass taught me just how empty life could be without scruples.
6. Failure to recognize East/West incompatibility taught me to read the fine print.
7. A lack of well-defined expectations taught me the benefits of clear communication.
8. Failing to appreciate the culture of an entire industry taught me to look before I leap.
9. Failure to focus on my family taught me how precious my loved ones are.
10. Thinking that people are inherently bad taught me not to make sweeping judgements.
11. Failure to take the initiative taught me that difficult conversations are necessary even if they aren't pleasant.
12. Failure to trust my gut taught me to listen to my own better judgment.

Additionally, leadership is about having a position and building a relationship through pragmatic efforts. Once you've got your head around a plan, once you've communicated it, then you go ahead and try it out. Sure, some attempts might flop, but those failures are your best teachers, provided you talk about them. The problem is that people tend to hide their failures. They're worried about their reputation, or they don't want their boss or shareholders to know they messed up. So, they sweep it under the rug.

And you know, that's a big part of the whole book right there. People don't talk about their failures openly. Especially in today's social media crazed environment where cancel culture and the ever search for "likes" are the basis of many actions, some are afraid of looking bad, so they keep quiet. Take the example of going after that car dealership. I should've communicated that I didn't know much about that industry and needed some help. But instead, I kept it to myself and guess what? I failed.

Within the four styles of leadership (positional, relational, pragmatic, and mentorship) there is a growth curve. You can't jump to mentorship without building relationships and trying things at the pragmatic level. The pragmatic leadership level emphasizes the process of trying things together...to build trust. Last, but not least, the mentorship level is all about trust and providing information freely to one another to help each party grow. And, you can't do any of this without communication. Having crucial and critical communications is key. It's all interconnected.

This book is for the next generation of leaders who have grown up in the handheld, social media construct. The key to perseverance through multiple failures and mastering actionable leadership is to communicate in-person, more often, and across reporting lines. Everything that must be said should be delivered seven times in four different formats. Do this and success will inevitably follow. What I want future leaders to understand is that fear is a natural part of the process. We all have it.

Hence, "Daring to Fail" means facing those fears head-on and not dragging out any significant change that needs to be made. The longer you wait, the scarier it gets. And another thing, especially for those dealing with private equity or external funding, don't be afraid to push back. Stand your ground. Take your shot. Sure, you might miss, and yes, you might even get fired. But if you don't take that swing, you're stuck with a mediocre outcome.

In all, you've got to dare to move forward, even if it means failing. Take that swing, push back, and don't let fear paralyze you. Failure isn't the end of the road; it is just the beginning. Communicate first, then, make every single one of those spectacular failures count!

SOURCES

"About Us," McDonald's. *https://www.mcdonalds.com/us/en-us/about-us.html*

"About West Point," United States Military Academy: West Point. *https://www.westpoint.edu/leadership-center/mcdonald-leadership-conference/about-west-point*

"Admissions FAQs," United States Military Academy at West Point. *https://www.westpoint.edu/admissions/frequently-asked-questions*

"Agents on I-15 Intercept $600K of China White Heroin," U.S. Customs and Border Enforcement. October 10, 2014. *https://www.cbp.gov/newsroom/local-media-release/agents-i-15-intercept-600k-china-white-heroin*

"AH-64 Apache," Boeing. *https://www.boeing.com/defense/ah-64-apache/*

"Banting Before Insulin," *ArcGIS StoryMaps*. *https://storymaps.arcgis.com/stories/e89951b374cb4b82848b9b1092d0b01c*

"Bill Hewlett and Dave Packard," *https://www.hewlettpackardhistory.com/collection/bill-hewlett-and-dave-packard/*

"Confrontation in the Gulf: U.S. to Sell Saudis $20 Billion in Arms; Weapons Deal Is Largest in History," *The New York Times*. September 15, 1990. *https://www.nytimes.com/1990/09/15/world/confrontation-gulf-us-sell-saudis-20-billion-arms-weapons-deal-largest-history.html*

"Difference Between General Officers and Flag Officers," Officer Assignments. *https://officerassignments.com/difference-between-general-officers-and-flag-officers/*

"Frederick Banting (1891-1941): Discoverer of insulin." *Singapore Medical Journal* vol. 58,1 (2017): 2-3. *https://www.ncbi.nlm.nih.gov/pmc/articles/PMC5331123/*

"Gain the Advantage With a Full-Tuition Scholarship: U.S. Military Academy at West Point," U.S. Army. *https://www.goarmy.com/careers-and-jobs/find-your-path/army-officers/military-academy.html*

"Gilded Age," history.com *https://www.history.com/topics/19th-century/gilded-age*

"Helping Veterans and Organizations Exceed their Potential," Lucas Group. *https://www.lucasgroup.com/military-transition/jobs/*

"Hewlett-Packard's Executive Leadership," *https://www.hewlettpackardhistory.com/executive-leadership/*

"Horace Greeley: 'Go West,' 1871," The Gilder Lehrman Institute of American History 2009-2019. *Period 5: 1848-1877 (AP US History) | Gilder Lehrman Institute of American History*

"How To Wire A 66 Block," *Tom Builds Stuff. https://tombuildsstuff.blogspot.com/2015/02/how-to-wire-66-block.html*

"John Malone to Restructure Liberty Media, Liberty Interactive," Reuters. November 12, 2015. *https://www.reuters.com/article/liberty-media-stock/update-3-john-malone-to-restructure-liberty-media-liberty-interactive-idUSL3N13749F20151113*

"Macallan 20 Year Old Masters of Photography Albert Watson Speyside Single Malt Scotch Whisky | 700ML," Cask Cartel. *https://caskcartel.com/products/macallan-20-year-old-masters-of-photography-albert-watson-speyside-single-malt-scotch-whisky-700ml?variant=34986499473546&utm_medium=cpc&utm_source=google&utm_campaign=Google Shopping&gclid=CjOKCQjw_r6hBhDdARIsAMIDhV8wb1Ko9ifgexqcfc_Ogel5LnJ2_eILG8FwpeTSOmo2ogjqmtYSuuIaArpWEALw_wcB*

"Money Ruining Marriages in America," Ramsey Solutions. February 6, 2018. *https://www.ramseysolutions.com/company/newsroom/releases/money-ruining-marriages-in-america*

"Nearly Half the World Lives on Less than $5.50 a Day," The World Bank. October 17, 2018. *https://www.worldbank.org/en/news/press-release/2018/10/17/nearly-half-the-world-lives-on-less-than-550-a-day*

"NexusTek Acquires Cal Net Technology Group, Syndeo Technologies and Decision Consultants, Inc.," *NexusTek*. *https://www.nexustek.com/news/nexustek-acquires-cal-net-technology-group-syndeo-technologies-and-decision-consultants-inc/*

"NexusTek Inc," Net App. *https://www.netapp.com/partners/partner-connect/nexustek-inc/*

"Notable Graduates," United States Military Academy: West Point. *https://www.westpoint.edu/about/history-of-west-point/notable-graduates*

"Quotes from *Boiler Room* (2000): Jim Young (Ben Affleck)," IMDB. *https://www.imdb.com/title/tt0181984/quotes/?ref_=tt_trv_qu*

"Railroads in the Late 19th Century: U.S. History Primary Source Timeline," Library of Congress. *https://www.loc.gov/classroom-materials/united-states-history-primary-source-timeline/rise-of-industrial-america-1876-1900/railroads-in-late-19th-century/*

"Sam Walton Biography – Everything to Know about the Walmart Founder," *Entrepreneur*. *https://www.entrepreneur.com/growing-a-business/sam-walton-biography/197560*

"Sara Lee: Classic Pound Cake," Sara Lee. *https://saraleedesserts.com/products/product-details/classic-pound-cake*

"Search Fund," Corporate Finance Institute. January 18, 2023. *https://corporatefinanceinstitute.com/resources/career/search-fund*

"Sputnik Launched," *History.com*. *https://www.history.com/this-day-in-history/sputnik-launched*

"*The Founder*: Quotes," *Internet Movie Database*. *https://www.imdb.com/title/tt4276820/quotes/?ref_=tt_trv_qu*

"Top Ten Crooked CEOS: Joe Nacchio," *Time*. https://content.time.com/time/specials/packages/article/0,28804,1903155_1903156_1903146,00.html

"Wendy Gramm," Frontline (PBS). https://www.pbs.org/wgbh/pages/frontline/president/players/gramm.html

Bankston, John. *Alexander Fleming and the Story of Penicillin*. (Unlocking the Secrets of Science). Bear, DE: Mitchell Lane, 2001.

Brandt, Richard. "Birth of a Salesman," *The Wall Street Journal*. October 15, 2011. https://www.wsj.com/articles/SB10001424052970203914304576627102996831200

Bulkeley, William. "A Data-Storage Titan Confronts Bias Claims," *The Wall Street Journal*. September 12, 2007. https://www.wsj.com/articles/SB118955478194424452

Burden, Lisa. "Dell EMC to pay $2.9M to settle gender, race pay discrimination charges," *HR Dive*. May 24, 2018. https://www.hrdive.com/news/dell-emc-to-pay-29m-to-settle-gender-race-pay-discrimination-charges/524208/

Cafarella, Haley. "The Importance of the Colonel Sanders Story," *FranchiseWire*. March 27, 2022. https://www.franchisewire.com/the-colonel-sanders-story/

Corfield, Garett. "Former HP CEO Léo Apotheker tells court he didn't read Autonomy's latest accounts before fated $11bn buyout," *The Register*. April 1, 2019. https://www.theregister.com/2019/04/01/leo_apotheker_autonomy_trial/

De Luce, Ivan. "11 Reasons Why It's Taking You So Long To Succeed in Life," Business Insider. May 31, 2019. https://www.businessinsider.com/reasons-why-its-taking-you-so-long-to-succeed-2019-5#youre-not-doing-the-tasks-that-count-1

Fitz-Gibbon, Jorge. "'Grit' More Important to Success than Brains and Brawn…" *New York Post*. November 4, 2019. https://nypost.com/2019/11/04/grit-more-important-to-success-than-brains-and-brawn-west-point-study-finds/

Garnett, Ley. "Enron's Last Remaining Firm Under Investigation," NPR. February 15, 2006. *https://www.npr.org/templates/story/story.php?storyId=5213518*

Gill, Michael. "A History of Stone Lifting and Strongman," Barbend. July 20th, 2023. *https://barbend.com/strongman-stone-history/*

Glei, Dana A, and Maxine Weinstein. "Drug and Alcohol Abuse: the Role of Economic Insecurity." *American Journal of Health Behavior* vol. 43,4 (2019): 838-853. doi:10.5993/AJHB.43.4.16. *https://www.ncbi.nlm.nih.gov/pmc/articles/PMC6631323/*

Glionna, John M. "Midshipman Recalls Her Rough Seas at Annapolis..." *The Los Angeles Times.* May 23, 1990. *https://www.latimes.com/archives/la-xpm-1990-05-23-me-86-story.html*

Grabel, Sam. "The Breakup of the Bell System," *The History Factory.* January 24, 2022.

Haden, Jeff. "64 Years Ago, Ray Kroc Made a Decision That Completely Transformed McDonald's. The Rest Is History," *Inc.* November 18, 2020. *https://www.inc.com/jeff-haden/64-years-ago-ray-kroc-made-a-decision-that-completely-transformed-mcdonalds-rest-is-history.html*

Hanford, Emily. "Angela Duckworth and the Research on '*Grit,*'" American Public Media. August 2012. *https://americanradioworks.publicradio.org/features/tomorrows-college/grit/angela-duckworth-grit.html*

Klein, Christopher. "8 Things You May Not Know About the Real Colonel Sanders," *History.com.* August 7, 2019. *https://www.history.com/news/8-facts-real-colonel-sanders-kfc*

Kumar, Jayant. "13 Business Leaders Who Failed Before They Succeeded," LinkedIn. May 14, 2016. *https://www.linkedin.com/pulse/13-business-leaders-who-failed-before-succeeded-jayant-kumar*

Lawless, Aaron. Maj. "Heard, Understood, Acknowledged," *Army University Press.* May 2023. *https://www.armyupress.army.mil/journals/military-review/online-exclusive/2023-ole/heard-understood-acknowledged/*

Lee, Jennifer., PhD. "The "Asian F": Perils of a Model Minority," *The Society Pages*. December 18, 2013. https://thesocietypages.org/socimages/2013/12/18/asian-fs-and-the-idea-of-asian-achievement/?amp;co=f000000009816s-1158206718

McCullough, Brian. "A revealing look at the dot-com bubble of 2000 — and how it shapes our lives today," TED: Ideas. Dec 4, 2018. *https://ideas.ted.com/an-eye-opening-look-at-the-dot-com-bubble-of-2000-and-how-it-shapes-our-lives-today/*

Mehta, Stephanie N. "Still Afloat In An Ocean Of Doubt," *CNN Money*. November 13, 2000. *https://money.cnn.com/magazines/fortune/fortune_archive/2000/11/13/291579/index.htm*

Meisenzah, Mary. "Starting in a garage is crucial to the origin story of many Silicon Valley entrepreneurs," *Business Insider*. April 1, 2020. *https://www.businessinsider.com/google-apple-hp-microsoft-amazon-started-in-garages-photos-2019-12*

Miller, Hannah L. "5 Levels of Leadership: Which Stage Have You Reached?" *Leaders*. September 7, 2022. *https://leaders.com/articles/leadership/5-levels-of-leadership/*

Miller, Ron. "$67 billion Dell-EMC deal closes today," TechCrunch. September 7, 2016. *https://techcrunch.com/2016/09/07/67-billion-dell-emc-deal-becomes-official-today/?guccounter=1&guce_referrer=aHR0cHM6Ly93d3cuZ29vZ2xlLmNvbS8&guce_referrer_sig=AQAAAL21_j3thFGdGFCYNa9oFSSF4lLYtWxflaufvPXSRItk QqkcZfolhxQ-NPFpVKcHLn0WPqkr28Odo4CSR8AMIPEWgWCr Z8EJCD-3JsqaAkNefdznh8SODpumzBcIfJamwfcBCXytjUPGwo_EeswqNfNC2sP71Vvexnz48mZD982K*

Morgan, Jacob. "Why You Should Have An Immigrant Mentality," *LinkedIn*. February 1, 2022. *https://www.linkedin.com/pulse/why-you-should-have-immigrant-mentality-jacob-morgan?trk=pulse-article_more-articles_related-content-card*

O'Donnell, Peggy. "The Politics of Pie Cutting at West Point's Mess Hall," *Atlas Obscura*. June 27, 2017. *https://www.atlasobscura.com/articles/west-point-mess-hall-pie*

Park, Nathan S. "South Korea's Nostalgia for Dictatorship Has (Mostly) Predictable Results," Foreign Policy. November 15, 2016. https://foreignpolicy.com/2016/11/15/south-koreas-nostalgia-for-dictatorship-has-mostly-predictable-results/

Pramuk, Jacob. "Police: McClendon Crashed Traveling at 'High Rate of Speed,'" CNBC. March 4, 2016. https://www.cnbc.com/2016/03/02/ex-chesapeake-ceo-mcclendon-dies-in-car-wreck-day-after-indictment.html

Robinson Jr., Clarence A. "Gulf War: Apache Raid," *Defense Media Network*. February 2, 2011. https://www.defensemedianetwork.com/stories/gulf-war-apache-raid/

Stuart, Matthew. "How AT&T Conquered All Forms of Communication After the Government Forced It to Break Up," *Business Insider*. March 3, 2018.

Tan, Siang Yong, Jason Merchant and Yvonne Tatsumura. "Alexander Fleming (1881-1955): Discoverer of penicillin." *Singapore Medical Journal* vol. 56,7 (2015): 366-7. https://www.ncbi.nlm.nih.gov/pmc/articles/PMC4520913/

The Boiler Room Ben Affleck Speech. YouTube. https://www.youtube.com/watch?v=JfIKzReNDF4

Thibodeau, Patrick. "Closing of EDS Deal Brings HP Closer to Rivals," Computerworld. August 26, 2008. https://www.computerworld.com/article/2532883/closing-of-eds-deal-brings-hp-closer-to-rivals.html

Vincent, Matt. "Tutorial: How to punch down a 66 block," *Cabling Installation and Maintenance*. May 23, 2014. https://www.cablinginstall.com/design-install/article/16477637/tutorial-how-to-punch-down-a-66-block

Zapata, Kimberly. "Financial Stress Is a Leading Catalyst for Suicide — Here's How You Can Find Help," *Health*. August 25, 2021. https://www.health.com/money/financial-stress-suicide-risk

Made in the USA
Las Vegas, NV
30 June 2025

24251371R00125